Microsoft

WORD 2022

A Quick Step-By-Step Guide to All You Must Learn in

MS Word to be Confident, Stress-Free, and more Productive

ELIZABETH A.

COPYRIGHT

TABLE OF CONTENTS

CHAPTER 1: INTRODUCTION

Welcome to Microsoft Word 2022, an up-to-date guide that provides all you need to know about Microsoft Word to be relevant, confident, and highly productive. In this book, you will learn how to use the most useful and amazing features of MS Word without stress. You will learn how to create, edit, and format a document from scratch like a professional, how to work confidently and smartly with MS word top shortcut commands, how to conveniently insert and format pictures, shapes, tables, and charts, how to save, print, share and secure your document and many more.

Microsoft Word, popularly called **MS-Word** or **Word,** is a word processing application developed by Microsoft Corporation. Word is part of Microsoft Office Suite and was launched in **1983**. It competed with WordPerfect (the most popular word processor then) to become the world-leading word processor since the **1990s** till date. The latest office suite is **Office 2021 and Office 365**. It can run on Windows, macOS, iOS, and Android operating systems.

Most of the essential Microsoft Word features have been around for a while, and the basics are similar for most versions. Therefore, if you have an older version of Word, Word 2021, or Word 365 read on; you will significantly benefit from this book.

You can use MS Word to create, edit, format, save, and print various professional-looking personal and business documents like books, graphics, invoices, resumes, reports, letters, pictures, emails, invitations, catalogs, memos, certificates, newsletters, and many more. It has a friendly user interface and is very easy to use.

1.1 MS WORD MOST ESSENTIAL FEATURES

Microsoft Word is the most used word processor in the world. It has a range of use for various organizations, teachers, students, professionals, business owners and an individual. Having little knowledge of the application and consistently figuring things out can be stressful and time-wasting. Microsoft Word has many excellent features you may not know if you do not learn the skill. Learning the skill will make you save time, work smartly, and increase your productivity.

Some of the fantastic features of Word that you will learn include

- Styles for easy and quick document formatting.
- Themes to create a professional-looking document with just a click.
- Illustrations like images, shapes, SmartArt, etc. to beautify and communicate without stress.
- Tables and Charts for easy and quick presentation of data
- Find and Replace feature for quick navigation and editing of your work.
- Paste Special and Clipboard system
- Sort for easy data analysis
- Autocorrect feature, spelling and Grammar to create an error free document.
- Synonym function (Thesaurus) for flexible word usage.
- Automatic Table of Content and Table of figures to ease your stress.
- Hyperlinking
- Security features and **so many others.**

Read on as I quickly show you how to use the Word amazing features to save your time, reduce your stress, increase your productivity, eliminate your frustration, improve your competence, and make you a professional in less than 3hours.

1.2 GETTING STARTED

To start using MS word, you must have it installed on your computer or use it online. Some computers come with Microsoft Office preinstalled, but if you do not have it, you can get it following the steps below:

1.2.1 Buy MS Word

1. Open your web browser, e.g., Google Chrome.
2. Go to office website: www.office.com.
3. Click on **Get office** if you want an office or MS Word on your desktop and buy from the available options:

   • **Office 365 Family** and **Office 365 Personal**: You can share Office 365 Family with six people, while Office 365 Personal is limited to only one person. They are both the same in function, and both require continuous subscriptions. Office 365 is the best option for any user who wants access to all the up-to-date office apps and cloud services. It can run on windows 11, 10, 8, 7, and macOS.

   • **Office Home & Student 2021**: This is the latest version of office available for a one-time payment and contains only the essential apps (Word, Excel, PowerPoint, Access, Outlook, OneNote, Team, and Publisher). You can only use it on Windows 11, 10, and macOS.

4. Install Microsoft Office, and MS word is available on your desktop for use.

1.2.2 Use MS Word Freely

If you are not interested in buying Microsoft office, you can use it **freely** on the Microsoft official website. The Word online version is new and does not contain all the features in the desktop version. The website version cannot also work when there is no connectivity, making the offline/ desktop version a good choice.

3

To use MS word freely online;

- visit their website, www.office.com.
- sign in if you have an existing account or
- create a new one if you do not have one, and MS word will be available for your use.

1.3 OPENING AND PINNING MS WORD.

To open an MS word:

1. Type **Word** in your computer search bar.

2. Left-click on the word icon or **Open** to open a new MS word file.

3. You can also click any recent lists to open an already existing file.

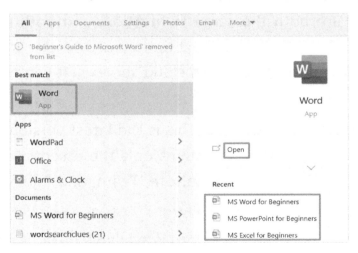

If you often use Word, it will be better to pin it to the start or taskbar.

To pin an MS Word to start or taskbar:

1. Right-click on the Word icon. A menu appears.
2. Select **Pin to Start** or **Pin to taskbar** as desired from the menu.

1.4 MS WORD START SCREEN

When you first open MS word, you will land on the start screen **Home** page, as shown below. The page has a blue vertical bar on the left side containing tabs to the right-side contents. The rest of the tabs have their shortcuts link on the **Home** page.

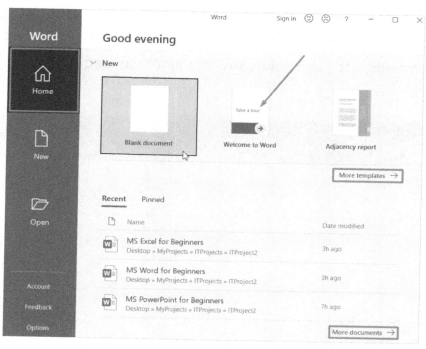

You have a **Blank** document on the **Home** screen that you can use to start from scratch. Also available are several learning tutorials and **templates** that can quickly get you started with MS Word. Click on more templates or the New tab at the left-hand bar if you want more templates.

Below the templates is the list of the **Recent** Word document. The **Open** tab at the left-sidebar or the **More documents** link opens more available documents at the right bottom corner of the list. Frequently open documents can be pinned and accessed in the **Pinned** beside the **Recent** list.

CHAPTER 2: GETTING TO KNOW WORD USER INTERFACE

2.1 WORD USER INTERFACE

Choosing a **blank document** in the Word start screen **Home** page opens up a Word document user interface. MS word work area has several bars, tabs, ribbons, commands, etc., as shown and explained subsequently.

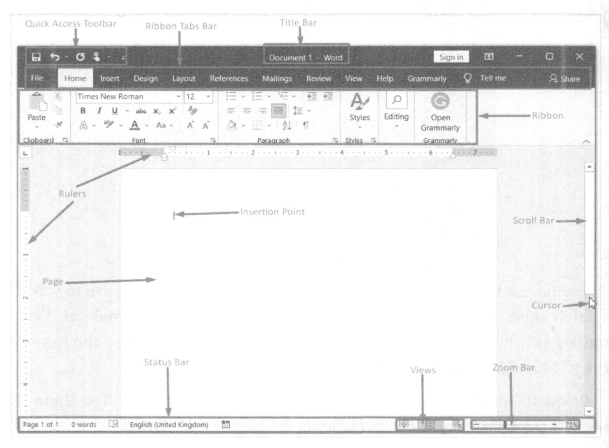

2.2 TITLE BAR

Title Bar shows the title of the document. Document 1 (and then Document 2, etc.)' is the Word default title name, and this can be changed when you save the document with your desired name.

To the far right of the title bar are window control buttons, as shown below:

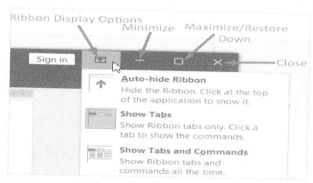

2.3 QUICK ACCESS TOOLBAR

The **Quick Access Toolbar** contains the icon list of all the most frequently used Word commands such as **Save, Undo, Redo, etc**.

2.3.1 Customizing Quick Access Toolbar

You can customize the quick access toolbar by adding your commonly used command.

To customize the quick access toolbar:

1. Click the drop-down button at the far right of the toolbar, check or uncheck any of the commands to add or remove it respectively as desired.

2. Or right-click on the desired command found in the **Home** ribbon or any other tab ribbons and select **Add to Quick Access Toolbar**.

   Alternatively,

1. Right-click on the quick access toolbar.

2. Select **Customize Quick Access Toolbar** from the listed option.

   Word Options dialog box appears.

3. Search and select the desired command(s) from the left-side pane.

4. Click the **Add** button.

5. Press **OK**.

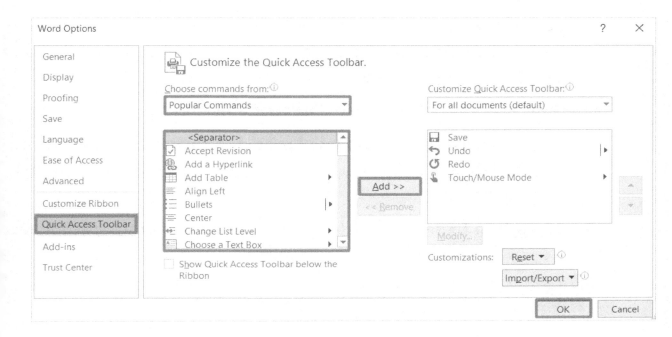

To remove any **Quick Access Toolbar** command, right-click on the tool and click on **Remove from Quick Access Toolbar** from the list.

2.4 THE RIBBON SYSTEM

MS Word has a lot of commands that are neatly arranged into the ribbon system. This system makes it easy to locate any command.

2.4.1 Ribbon Tabs, Groups, and Commands

The Ribbon system is tailored into three components:

- **Tabs:** These are buttons with descriptive names that allow the user to quickly find and use a group of commands to complete a specific task. Examples are Home, Insert, Design, Layout, References, Review, etc.

- Contextual Tabs - These tabs only appear when table, image, picture figures, chart, etc., are inserted or selected in the document. They are majorly used to design and format the selected object.

Each tab has its ribbon displayed below it when clicked.

- **Groups:** Ribbon contains **groups** of related commands or word features, e.g., the **Home** tab ribbon has **Clipboard** group, **Font** group, **Paragraph** group, and so on.

- **Commands:** These are Word feature buttons that perform a specific task.

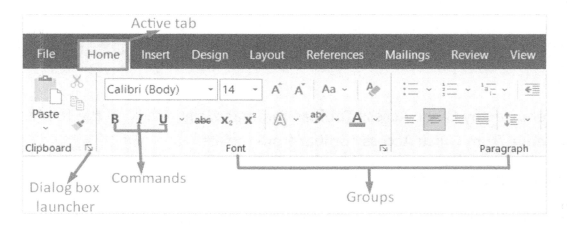

Most groups but not all have a **dialog box launcher** at their right-side bottoms for more group-related commands not available in the ribbon.

2.4.2 Customizing the Ribbon

You can remove or add any ribbon tabs, groups, and commands to suit your desire and work.

To customize the ribbon:

1. Right-click on the ribbon. A menu box appears.
2. Select **Customize the Ribbon.**

The **Word Options** dialog box appears.

3. Select an option from **Choose commands from the** drop-down button

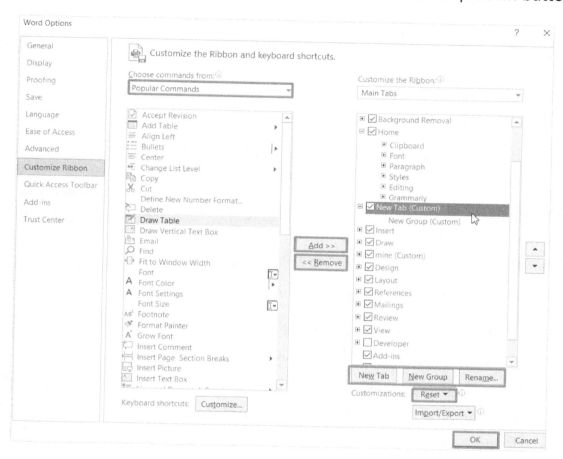

4. To create a new tab, click the **New Tab** button

   To add a new group to an existing tab, select the tab at the right-side pane and click the **New Group** button. Use the **Rename** buttons to rename your custom group or tabs.

   Note: You can only add commands to a custom group, i.e., you cannot add commands to the Word default groups.

5. Search and select the desired command(s) from the left-side pane.

6. Click the **Add** button or double-click on the command.

7. Press **OK**.

To remove a custom tab, group, and command, select it in the right-side pane and click the **Remove** button. You can reset all customization using the **Reset** button at any time.

2.5 BACKSTAGE VIEW

The Backstage View is the central managing place for all Word documents. To go to the backstage of the Word document, click on the **File** tab in the **Ribbon** Tabs bar.

You can create, save, open, print, or share your document from backstage. Starting from the top the:

- **New** allows you to open a new Word document.

- **Open** allows you to open the document you have created earlier from different locations.

- **Info** gives information about the Word document, allowing you to protect, inspect and manage your document.

- **Save** saves the current document with the same name and location.

- **Save as** will enable you to rename, select the desired location and save the recent document.

- **Print** allows you to print your document in the desired format.

- **Share** lets you share your document through email or online.

- **Export** allows you to create the PDF or XPS document of your Word document.

- **Account** contains all the document holder's details. You can change the look of your Office applications and do some other settings here.

- **Close** allows you to exit the current document. The Top-left-corner **arrow** will enable you to go back to the document area.

- **Options** opens the **Word Options** dialog box

2.5.1 Word Options

In Word Options, you can do all Word customizations and default settings. When clicked, most customized commands in Word bring up this same dialog box called Word Options.

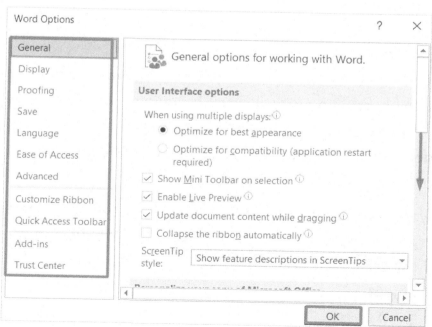

Come to this box if you think you need some changes to the default setting and customization of your Word. Select any option that seems related to what you desire to do in the left-side pane and make the settings at the right-side window.

2.6 DOCUMENT AREA

2.6.1 Page

The page is the white widow where all your input will be displayed. There i always a vertical blinking line on the page called **insertion point**. The insertion point indicates where text or anything you put into your document will be added You can relocate your insertion point to the desired place by moving your curso and double-clicking in the area.

Your document, when printed, will appear in the paper exactly the way i appears on the page.

2.6.2 Scroll Bars

There are two scroll bars in the Word document area, the vertical and horizontal scroll bars. The vertical scroll bar allows you to scroll your documen downward and upward, while the horizontal scroll bar will enable you to scrol your document left and right. The scroll bars only appear if all the documen pages cannot be displayed on the window.

To scroll your document page, left-click on the scroll bar, hold and drag down up, left, or right as the case may be. You can also left-click on the arrows at th terminals of the scroll bar, hold down for fast movement and click intermittentl for slow movement.

2.6.3 Rulers

Word has two rulers; a vertical and a horizontal ruler. The horizontal ruler is used for quick indent settings (to be discussed in full later).

2.7 STATUS BAR

The status bar contains specific information about the Word document or selected text. By default, the status bar contains the current page and total page numbers, word counts, language, zoom slider, and some page view icons.

2.7.1 Zoom Bar

- The zoom bar allows you to zoom in and out of the document to make your document page appears larger and smaller, respectively, as desired.
- Drag the slider either towards the right side (+) or left side (-) to zoom in and out, respectively. You can also click on the bar to position the slider.
- Click on + and – to increase or reduce the view with multiples of 10.
- Click on the percentage tab to open the zoom window to set the page view.
- You can only set the zoom between 10% and 500%.

2.7.2 Views

Views suggest ways to look at your files. There are three default view options available on the status bar: **normal**, **Page layout**, and **Page break preview.** More view options are available in the **View** tab.

2.7.3 Customizing the Status Bar

There are quite a number of information you can display on the status bar. You can customize the status bar for whatever information you desire, to do this;

- Right-click on the bar. A Dialog box appears.

- Check or uncheck an option as the case may be.

Customize Status Bar	
Formatted Page Number	16
Section	5
✓ Page Number	Page 24 of 145
Vertical Page Position	3.8"
Line Number	10
Column	1
✓ Word Count	20524 words
✓ Spelling and Grammar Check	Errors
✓ Language	English (United Kingdom)
✓ Label	
✓ Signatures	Off
Information Management Policy	Off
Permissions	Off
Track Changes	Off
✓ Caps Lock	Off
Overtype	Insert
Selection Mode	
✓ Macro Recording	Not Recording
Accessibility Checker	
✓ Upload Status	
✓ Document Updates Available	
✓ View Shortcuts	
✓ Zoom Slider	
✓ Zoom	96%

2.8 WORD CONTEXT HELP FEATURE.

This feature gives word users appropriate information about word commands to educate them about its work. To get information about a particular command:

- Hover on the command, i.e., take your cursor over the **command** and wait for a little.
- A context help widow describing the command will appear as shown below.
- Click the **Tell me more** link to learn more about the command on the Office website.

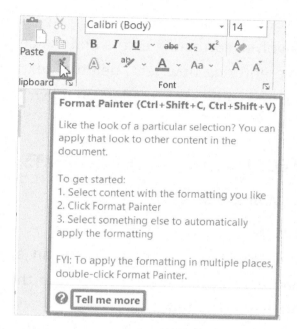

With this feature, you can know what all commands do in Word.

CHAPTER 3: CREATING AND EDITING DOCUMENTS.

You can create and edit your documents in MS Word with either a mouse, keyboard, or both. Creating a document involves typing using a keyboard, and editing a document involves correcting errors and making other desired changes. The techniques involve entering new text, deleting texts, changing texts, and so on. Written below are step-by-step guides on how to create and edit your document.

3.1 ENTERING, SELECTING, AND DELETING TEXTS

To Enter Texts into your Document:

1. Open your MS Word
2. Select a blank document, a template, or an existing document. Word automatically sets the text insertion point at the top of the first page of any newly opened document.
3. For existing document: Scroll down and click the point you want to enter new texts, like the last page, to reposition the insertion point.
4. Type your new texts using the keyboard, and the texts appear at the text insertion point.

Note:

- Press the space bar on your keyboard once to put space between words.
- Do not Press **Enter** button to move to the following line. Word automatically moves to the next line when the current line is filled.
- Press **the Enter button on your keyboard only when starting** a new paragraph.

- Word automatically creates a new page once the current one is filled.

To Select Texts in MS Word:

1. Put your cursor next to the texts you want to select.
2. Left-click your mouse, holding it down, move it across the texts.
3. Release the mouse.

OR

1. Click at the beginning of the texts you want to select.
2. Hold down the **Shift** button on your keyboard
3. Click at the end of the texts or **press** any of the arrow keys on your keyboard to select the texts in the direction of the arrow.

Some Shortcut ways of selecting Texts:

To select:

- **A word** – Double click on the word.
- **A line** – Place the mouse pointer at the left margin and click **once** in front of the line.
- **A sentence** – Press and hold the **Ctrl** button on your keyboard, then click anywhere on the sentence.
- **A paragraph** – Place the mouse pointer in the left margin and double click next to any paragraph line. You can also Triple-click anywhere in the paragraph.
- **The whole Document** – Press the **Ctrl** key, place your mouse pointer anywhere in the margin, and left-click once or triple-click anywhere in the margin. Alternatively,

   - Go to the **Home** tab, click on **Select** in **Editing** group, and **select all. OR**

- Press **Ctrl + A** on your keyboard.

To Select multiple texts that are not together:

Hold down the **Ctrl** button and use any of the methods above to select the texts one after the other.

To Delete Texts:

1. Highlight the texts you want to delete.
2. Press the **Delete** button on your keyboard

   OR

1. Place your cursor to the left side of the text you want to delete.
2. Press the **Delete** button on your keyboard.

   OR

1. Place your cursor to the right of the texts you want to delete
2. Press the **Backspace** button on your keyboard.

To replace texts:

1. Select the texts.
2. Type the new texts over it.

You do not need to delete the texts; Word automatically deletes the old selected texts and replaces them with the newly typed text.

3.2 CUT, COPY AND PASTE TEXTS

Cutting text removes the text from its initial position and places it where it is **Pasted** while **copying** reproduces the text in another place.

There are various ways of copying, cutting, and pasting texts in Word; some of the top ones include the following:

Method 1:

- Select the text you want to cut or copy.
- Click on the **Home** tab and select the Copy or Cut command as desired.
- Place your cursor to where you want to paste your text.
- Click on the **Paste** command in the **Home** tab.

Method 2:

- Select the texts you want to copy or cut.
- Right-click on the selected text.
- Select the **Copy** or **Cut** option from the menu that appears.
- Move your cursor to the desired location and right-click on your mouse.
- Select the **Paste** option with a left-click from a menu that appears.

Alternatively, you can use the shortcut commands:

- **Ctrl + C** to copy
- **Ctrl + X** to cut
- **Ctrl + V** or **Shift + Insert** to paste

Tips: You can use the **paste** option to paste the item you copied or cut last as many times and at many places as desired.

3.3 PASTE SPECIAL OPTIONS AND CLIPBOARD

Paste Special Options

While working on your document, you will most likely want to copy/cut some texts that already have formatting like font type, font size, color, etc. When you copy/cut these formatted texts into word, Word automatically reformats the texts to the destination format, which might not be what you want. However, Paste

Special Option is provided to help you retain the original format, paste the item as a link, picture, or plain text, depending on your choice.

Paste Special is a word feature that provides several format options to Paste your item. The format in which you can paste your texts includes Microsoft Word Object, Formatted text, Unformatted text, Picture, file, Html format, and Unformatted Unicode Text (UUT).

To use Paste Special Options:

- Copy or cut the item you want to paste, e.g., texts, picture, shape, slide etc.
- Click where you want to insert the item in your document.
- Go to the **Home** tab in the **Clipboard** group and click the dropdown arrow under **Paste.**
- Select **Paste Special** from the menu that comes up.

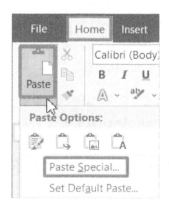

- Choose one of the options from the pop-up window as desired.

Alternatively, you can use the **Ctrl + Alt + V** shortcut command on your keyboard to call the **Paste Special** window.

Note: The **Paste Special** options change based on the item you want to paste.

Clipboard

Clipboard is the location where the cut or copy texts are temporarily stored and can be recalled for use with a **Paste** command. Microsoft has a multi-clipboard that can store up to 24 items copied or cut, unlike a window clipboard that can only hold one item at a time. The **Paste** command only recalls the last item copied or cut, and you can assess the other items by opening the clipboard.

To paste any of your copied items from the clipboard:

1. Go to **the Home** tab, under the **clipboard** group.
2. Click the expandable dialog box button to display the clipboard with the list of all the copied/cut items.

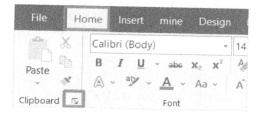

3. Click on the item of your choice to paste it at the insertion point or
4. Move your cursor to the item you want, and in front, you will see a drop-down button with options to paste or delete.

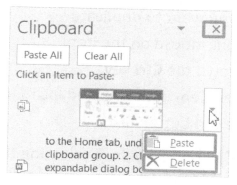

5. Select **Paste**, and your item will be inserted in the insertion point or **Delete** to remove the data from the clipboard if you do not need it again.

Click the **x** button to close the clipboard panel and **arrow** down options to change its location (move), resize, or close it as desired.

3.4 MOVING AND DUPLICATING

Moving removes the text or object from its initial position to another location, just like cut and paste while duplicating reproduces your text in another place like copy and paste. It is easier to move/duplicate than cut/copy and paste.

The difference between Cut/copy and move/duplicate is that while cut/copy stores their items in the clipboard, move/duplicate never does. Therefore, it is advisable to use the cut/copy and paste command if you need the item later because you can easily retrieve them on the clipboard.

To move your text:

- Select the texts or items you want to move.
- Click and hold your mouse
- drag and drop the item in the desired location.

To duplicate your text:

- Select the item you want to duplicate.
- Click and hold your mouse on the item.
- Press and hold down the **Ctrl** key.
- Drag and **drop** the item in the desired location.
- Then release the **Ctrl** button last.

Note: If you release the **Ctrl** button before releasing the item in the new location, the item will be moved and not duplicated.

3.5 UNDO, REDO, AND REPEAT

MS Word keeps track of most of your tasks while working on your document until you close the document. You can undo tasks like formatting, typing, deleting, etc., and some actions like clicking on command, saving your document, etc., you cannot undo. By default, Word can save up to **100** tasks you can undo.

To redo a task only a step back;

- Click on the undo icon 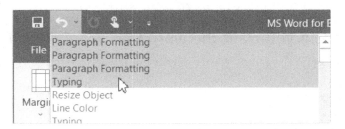 in the **Quick Access Toolbar** once
- or even more for more steps backward.

For many steps backward;

- Click on the dropdown button in front of the undo icon;
- a list of all the tasks you have performed since you open the document up to 100 appears.
- Select a point in the list, and Word will undo everything you have done to that point. You can only undo all the steps from the present to a point you select on the list. You cannot undo a single action that is not immediate.

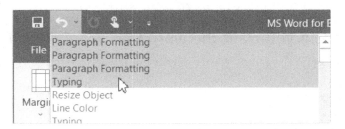

If you do not want to undo your task again, redo command is also available for you to use in the **Quick Access Toolbar**. If there is nothing to redo, Words change the redo icon to repeat icon for you to repeat some repeatable actions.

The redo and undo action command becomes inactive if there is nothing to undo or redo.

Keyboard Shortcuts:

Press **Ctrl + Z to undo.**

Press **Ctrl + Y to redo or repeat** as the case may be.

3.6 USING AUTOCORRECT IN WORD

Autocorrect is one of the amazing features of Word that fixes hundreds of common spelling errors and typos automatically. The correction happens instantly that you might not even notice it. For instance, you cannot type the word **hellp** because Word automatically corrects it to **help** by default.

Aside from typos and spelling errors, autocorrect features helps in fixing common punctuation mistakes, automatically capitalizing the first letter of any sentence, names of days, months, and some inverse capitalization errors.

Common text shortcuts are also autocorrected to their proper characters by this Word feature. For example, if you type -->, it automatically corrects to →, (R) changes to ®, the proper registered symbol, and so many in the list.

But what happens if you want the word that Word has autocorrected. You can undo the autocorrect.

To undo an AutoCorrect:

- Quickly press **Ctrl + Z** or undo before typing any other characters, and if you did not catch it fast,
- Move your cursor to the blue rectangle at the bottom of the first letter of any autocorrect word and click. A menu box appears to undo the autocorrect or do some other further settings.

appears

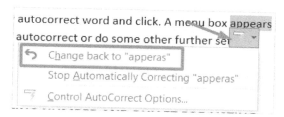

You can edit the Word autocorrect feature, add your own always misspelled word, or remove some words from autocorrecting.

To adjust AutoCorrect Settings:

1. Click the **File** tab to go to the **Backstage**.
2. Select **Options** in the left side menu bar. The **word Option** window appears.
3. Choose **Proofing** in the left side menu.

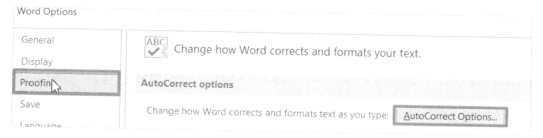

4. Click on the **AutoCorrect Options** button. An autoCorrect dialog box appears with the autocorrect tab active. Click on other tabs as desired.

    You will see the list of all problems that Word fixes for you from the dialog box.

5. Select and press the **Delete** button to remove anyone you do not want word to autocorrect.
6. Add a new entry using the **Replace** and **With** text boxes.

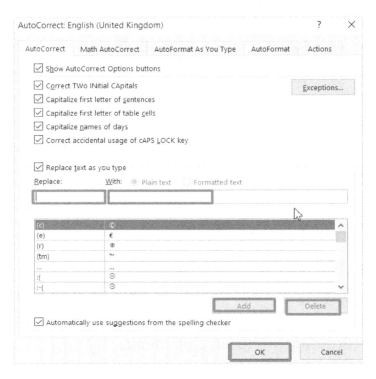

7. Press the **OK** button and close the dialog box.

3.7 PUTTING NUMBERS AND BULLETS FOR LISTING

Word allows you to organize your content using numbered or bulleted lists. Bullet/number makes your list distinct and easy to read. You can customize your list by editing or formatting the bullet/number font, color, icon style, and alignment.

A numbered list is used when the order of items in your list matters, and bulleted lists when the order of items in your list does not matter. There is also a **Multilevel** listing that can either be bulleted or numbered. You can put an outline of topics or subtopics in your document together by multilevel listing

To create a bulleted list:

1. Highlight the list you want to add a bullet to **or**

28

Place the cursor where you want the bullet to be.

2. Go to the **Home** tab, then to the **Paragraph** group.

3. Click on the **Bullets** icon to use the most recently applied Bullets style or the bullet dropdown button to change the style. ⊟ ⌄

   A **Bullet Library** dialog box appears with the list of bullets styles.

4. Select your desired bullet style,

   And it appears in your document.

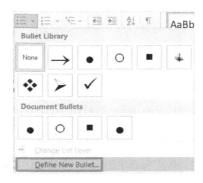

To customize your list bullet:

5. Select **Define New Bullet...**

   A Define New Bullet dialog box appears.

6. Set the **character** and **alignment** as desired, then press **OK**

   - Select **Symbol** to use a symbol as your listing icon. A symbol dialog box appears, choose your desired symbol, press OK, and your symbol is set as your listing icon.

   - Select **Picture** to use an online picture or any picture on your computer as a list icon.

   - Select **Font** to set the **font style**, the **font size,** and the **effects** of your list icons.

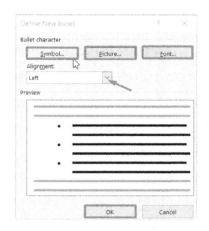

To create a numbered list:

1. Highlight the list you want to add numbers to **or**
   Place the cursor where you want the numbering to be.
2. Go to the **Home** tab, then in the **Paragraph** group,
3. Click on the **Numbering** icon  to apply the last recent numbering style or the dropdown button to change the style.

   A **Numbering Library** dialog box appears with the list of numbering styles.
4. Select your desired numbering style, and it appears in your document.

To customize your numbered list:

5. Select **Define New Number Format...**
   A **Define New Number Format** dialog box appears.
6. Select and set the **forma**t **/alignment** as desired.

If your cursor is already in numbered or bulleted lists, selecting bullets or the numbering command will change the list style.

Also available is a **Multilevel list** command  for you to use if your list has sub list.

You can format the listing style by right-clicking on the list and selecting an option as desired.

	Adjust List Indents...
↓≡	Restart at 1
	Continue Numbering
	Set Numbering Value...

3.8 INSERTING SYMBOLS, SPECIAL CHARACTERS, AND EQUATIONS

You cannot find some valuable symbols and characters on the keyboard. These symbols and characters are available as part of Word features. Also available are some common and complex predefined equations that can make your work easy.

To insert such symbol or special character;

1. Position your cursor where you want to insert the symbol.
2. Go to the **Insert** tab in the **Symbols** group.
3. Click on **Symbol**. A dropdown menu appears.

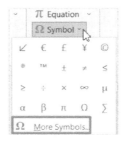

4. Select the desired symbol if found on the list; otherwise, click on **More Symbols** for more available options.

5. Select your desired symbol.

6. Click **insert**. The symbol will appear in your document.

7. Then Close the **Symbol** window.

For Special characters:

1. Click the **Special Character** tab in the **Symbol** window (follow steps 1-4 above to open it)

2. Click on the desired character and click the **Insert** button.

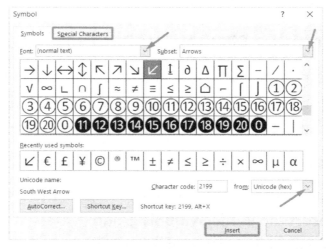

There are so many symbols that you can use in this feature. You can change the **font** and the **subset** to view them. Also displayed in the dialog box are the Unicode name and the character name of the selected symbol. You can familiarize yourself with the symbols by changing the font and the subset for you to locate anyone when needed quickly.

To insert Built-in Equations:

1. Position your cursor where you want to insert the equation.
2. Go to the **Insert** tab in the **Symbols** group.
3. Click on the **Equation** dropdown button for the list of the equations.

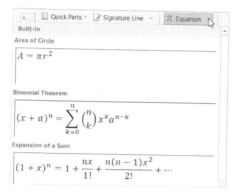

4. Select the desired equation to insert it.
5. Design and add to the equation from the **Equation Tools Design** tab that appears as desired.

You can click on the **Equation** command to insert an empty equation frame that you can build up into your desired equation. Word provides a contextual equation tools tab for easy design of the equation. This contextual equation tools tab is an amazing feature to make working with equations easy.

3.9 HYPERLINKING TEXT

Hyperlinking a text turns the text into a link and makes it clickable. The link, when clicked, jumps to another location, either in the document or a different location outside the document like a website, another file, a new email message, or any other place the text is being hyperlinked to. This feature is perfect for easy navigation of your document.

MS word, automatically convert a web address to a hyperlink when you type the address and press **Enter** or **Spacebar** after the address, e.g., www.office.com

To turn your text into a Hyperlink:

1. Select the text you want to turn to a link.
2. Go to the **Insert** tab, under **Links** group. You can also right-click on the text: A menu appears.
3. Click the **Link** command.
4. Select the link destination and fill in the required information in the **Insert Hyperlink** window that pops up. There are four available options to choose from based on what you want:

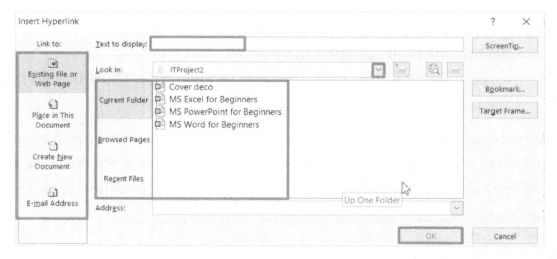

- Select **Existing File or Web Page** to link your text to a website or file And enter the URL in the address text box or choose from other options.

- Select **Place in this Document** and choose the location from the available list by the right to link your text to the area in the same document.
- Select **Create New Document** to link your text to create a new document. Enter the new document name in the **Name of New Document** textbox, Click **change** in the **full path** section to change the new document location, and choose whether you want to edit the document now or later in the **When to edit** section.
- Select **Email Address** to link the text to send an email to a recipient. Enter the email address or choose from the recently used address.

5. Enter **Ok** to apply, and the text now appears as a link.

To follow a link in MS word.

- Click and hold the **Ctrl** button.
- Click on the link, and it will take you to its destination.

You can edit the link by right-clinking on it and choosing from the menu that appears, based on what you want to do.

Word formats hyperlinked text differently from all other texts by default, and you can change the setting in the **Word Options.**

3.10 USING FIND AND REPLACE IN WORD

Find command is a word feature that allows you to find text in your document. The Replace option is also available in Word, **which will enable you to find words and** replace the words with other words.

3.10.1 Using the Find feature in Word.

Find command can search through your document in seconds and find for you a word, phrase, pages, headings, and even a character. You can search through either a section of your document or the entire document.

To find text:

1. Go to the **Home** tab.
2. Click the **Find** button in the **Editing** group. A Navigation pane appears on the left side of the window.
3. Click and type in the navigation pane textbox the word or phrase you want to search.
4. Press Enter. The Navigation pane brings the list of all the matching text.
5. Select any of the displayed text.
6. Click the X button in the upper-right corner of the pane to close the pane.

3.10.2 How to streamline your search

Word also provides you with a way of customizing your search to eliminate too many irrelevant findings.

To customize your search:

1. Go to the **Home** tab.
2. Click the **Find** button in the **Editing** group.
   A **Navigation** pane appears.

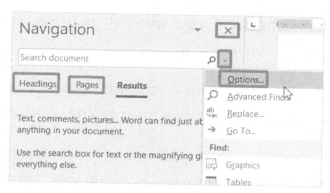

3. Click on the drop-down button to the far right of the search textbox. A menu box appears.

4. Select **Options**.

   A **Find Options** window appears.

5. Check all the desired options in the window.

   - Select **Match case** if you want the text in the exact case you typed, i.e., searching for **Learn** will not bring **learn** if you select this option.

   - Select **Find Whole Words Only** if you want text that is not part of another word, i.e., searching for '**in**' will not find '**instance**'.

   - Select **Use Wildcards** if you want to search for some words that you are not sure of their middle characters. Use the single character (?) and multiple **characters** (*) wildcards to search, i.e., search for **r?t** to bring **rut, rot, rat, ret.** Also, search for **r*t** to get **rust, roast,** and the likes.

   - Select **Sounds like** if you want texts that also sound like the text you typed. i.e., searching for **fat** will bring **fat, fart,** and the likes.

   - Select **Find All Word Forms** if you want all variants of the text, i.e., searching for only **write** will bring **write, wrote, written, writing.**

Select **Highlight All** if you want all matches of your search to b
color-filled, i.e., highlighted.

- Select **Incremental Find** if you want a continuous highlight of you
text as you type and not only after typing your search.

- Select **Match Prefix** if you want text that contains the prefix yo
type. i.e., searching for **un** will bring **unable** and others.

- Select **Match Suffix** if you want text that contains the suffix yo
type, i.e., searching for er brings getter, dancer, and the likes

- Select **Ignore Punctuation characters** if you want to find the text
that match yours, even if the text contains some punctuations. i.e
searching for **beginners** will also bring **beginner's**.

- Select **Ignore White-space characters** if you want to find the text
that match yours even if the text contains extra spaces. i.e
searching for **stepbystep** will also bring **step by step.**

6. Click the **OK** button to close the window.

In the Navigation pane that appears when you follow **steps 1-2** above, ther
are options to search through the headings and pages of your document.

- To search through your document's headings, click on **Headings** in th
Navigation pane and select from the list of all the headings. Word open
the page where the header is located.
- To search through the pages of your document, Click on **Pages** in th
Navigation pane. Word turns all the pages of your document int
thumbnails. Select your desired page, and word opens the page.

3.10.3 Using the Find and Replace Command in Word.

Word provides you an option to find a text and replace the text with a desired one.

To find and replace text:

1. Go to the **Home** tab
2. Click on **Replace** button in the **Editing** group.
   Find and Replace dialog box appears. You can also use **Ctrl + H** to launch this box.
3. Click in the **Find What** text box and type the texts you want to search.
4. Click in the **Replace With** textbox and input the text to replace the text you put in the **Find What** box.
   For more **Find** options, click the **More** button, and select any additional option.
5. Select any of the following buttons:
   - **Replace** to replace the currently highlighted text.
   - **Replace All** to replace all matches in the entire document.
   - **Find Next** to replace all the matches, starting from the current cursor position to the end of the document.

Word automatically replaces the word or phrase

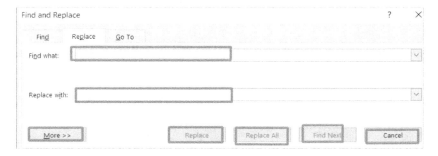

6. To close the dialog box, Click the cancel button or **X** icon at the top of the dialog box.

3.11 HOW TO SORT IN WORD

Sort is one of MS Word's handy features you can use to arrange your work in alphabetical or numerical order. It is especially useful if you are trying to organize your data in a table, and it can also arrange paragraphs or lists as the case maybe.

To sort your work:

1. Select the list you want to sort.
2. Go to the **Home** tab.
3. Click on the **Sort** icon in the **Paragraph** group.

A **Sort** dialog box appears that lets you sort your list or table on up to three levels of numbers, text, or dates either in ascending or descending order.

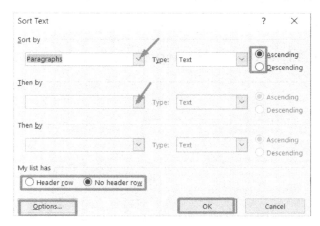

4. Set the dialog box as desired.
   - Set **Sort by** to:

- **Paragraph** if you want to sort the list by paragraph
- **Headings** if you're going to sort list that has headings
- **Field** if you're going to sort the list by field. Define your field in the **Options** button.
- **Headers** name if working with a table that has headers.
- **Columns number** if working with the table without headers.

- Set **Type** to Text, Number, or Date depending on what you want to sort.

- Set the sorting method: **Ascending or Descending**.

- Set **My List has** radio buttons. Choose whether your list or table has headers or no headers.

5. Press **Ok**.

3.12 CHECKING SPELLING AND GRAMMAR.

Microsoft Word, by default, automatically checks for incorrect spelling and grammar errors as you type your document. You can turn the feature on or off in the Word Options in the **Proofing** tab.

- Words that have spelling errors have wavy red underlines.
- Words that do not fit the context of the sentence have double-blue underlines.
- Grammar errors have wavy green underlines.

To check for spelling and grammar:

1. Go to the **Review** tab.
2. Select the **Spelling & Grammar** button in the **Proofing** group.
   A **Proofing** navigation pane appears, highlighting the first error in your document. The **Proofing** navigation pane states the issue with the word or phrase and gives you suggestions and other options.

3. Select an option.
   - Click on the **Suggestions** to accept it.
   - Click **Ignore Once** if you think the word is correct or want it the way it is.
   - Select **Don't check for this issue** if you want to ignore all the occurrence of the word.
   - Select **Options for "the issue"** if you want to open Word Options to customize the proofing for that issue.
   The proofing pane brings the second error in your document.
4. Repeat step 3 as you move through the whole document.
5. To close the Proofing navigation pane, click on the **X** button at the right-top corner of the pane.

You can also right-click on the underlined words and select either the suggestion or ignore options.

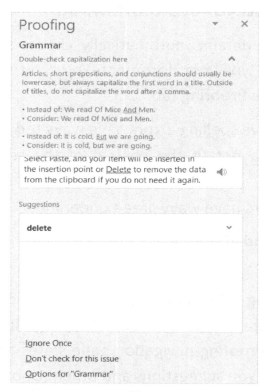

3.13 THESAURUS.

Thesaurus helps you find a word that is similar to your chosen word. It suggests different ways of saying what you want to say.

To use Thesaurus:

1. Select the word you want its synonyms.
2. Go to the **Review** tab.
3. Click on **Thesaurus**.

    A Thesaurus navigation pane appears at the right-side, containing the list of all the synonyms.

4. Move your cursor to a word that appeals to you.

    You can scroll up and down to see the complete list.
5. Click on the dropdown arrow at the right of the word.

    A menu appears.
6. Select **Insert** to replace your word with the word or

    Select **Copy** to save it on the clipboard for later use.

Alternatively,

1. Select the word you want its synonyms.
2. Right-click on the word. A dropdown list appears.
3. Select **Synonyms**. A word list menu appears.
4. Select a word that appeals to you, or select **Thesaurus** for a more word list.

CHAPTER 4: WORKING WITH TABLES AND CHARTS

4.1 INSERTING A TABLE

Table enables you to conveniently display and organize your bulky information clearly.

To insert a Table:

1. Position your cursor where you want the table to be.
2. Click **Insert** tab.
3. Select **Table** in the **Tables** group.
   Insert Table drop-down appears
4. Drag your mouse along the small boxes to highlight the number of rows and columns you want in your table.
   Your table appears simultaneously in the document as you highlight.

Alternatively;

1. Select **Insert Table...** in the **Insert Table** drop-down.
   Insert Table window appears.
2. Specify the number of rows and columns in the **Table Size** fields.
3. Check the AutoFit behavior buttons as desired.
4. Set whether to remember the dimensions for another table or not.
5. Click **OK**.

4.2 DRAWING A TABLE

Drawing your table with a drawing tool gives you flexibility when inserting your table. You can draw your table when you want to insert a table that is not uniform like the table below:

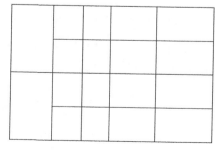

To draw a Table:

1. Go to the **Insert** tab.
2. Click **Table** in the **Tables** group.
3. Select **Draw Tables** in the drop-down that appears.
   Your mouse turns to a drawing tool.
4. Move your mouse into your document.
5. Drag your mouse into your desired size to draw the outer box of you table.
6. Draw each line of the rows and columns into the box as desired.
7. Press the **Esc** button on your keyboard when done.

4.3 EDITING A TABLE

You can always edit your table after you have created it. Below are step-by step guides on how to move around and edit your table.

4.3.1 Moving within a Table

The way you move the insertion point and select text in a table is somehow the same as how you do to text in the Word document. However, some methods are specific to the table, and they are as follow

To move within the table:

- Use the **Tab** key to move from left to right in a row.
- Use the **Shift + Tab** key to move from right to left in a row.
- Double-click in a cell to place the insertion point in the cell.
- **To select a single cell**: Drag over the cell content or click three times in the cell.

- **To select an entire row:** Click the left margin of the row, or drag your cursor across the whole row contents.
- **To select an entire column**: Click the column's top border or drag across the column's content.
- **To select the entire table**: Click on the table icon ⊞ at the top left corner of the table or press the **Alt** key and double click in any of the table cells.

4.3.2 Inserting Rows and Columns in a Table

To insert rows or columns to your table

1. Click in the row or column next to which you want to insert a new one.
2. Select the **Layout** tab in the contextual **Table Tools** tab that appears.
3. Click on **Insert Above** or **Insert Below**, or **Insert Left** or **Insert Right** based on where you want the new row/column regarding your current location.

Alternatively, you can draw another row or column directly into the table following the steps below:

1. Click within the table.
   The contextual table tabs appear.
2. Click the **Layout** tab
3. Select **Draw** table.
   Your cursor turns to a drawing tool.
4. Draw anywhere as desired in your new column or row.

Shortcut method:

1. Move your cursor to the left or top boundary of the table
   a circled plus sign appears

2. Click on it to add a new row down or a new column to the right.

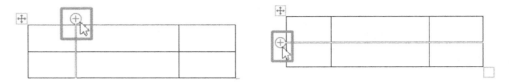

4.3.3 3 Ways of Adjusting Column and Row Sizes

When inserting your table, Word automatically creates the rows and columns of the table with uniform sizes. Sometimes there is a need to adjust the size of the columns and rows as needs arise.

There are many ways by which you can resize table rows or columns.

To adjust the column or row width using the mouse;

1. Position your cursor on the column or row boundary.
   The cursor changes to double lines with arrows at both sides

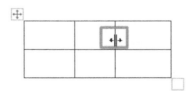

2. Drag the cursor to the direction you want to change the size.
3. Release the mouse when you are done.

To adjust the column or row size using AutoFit.

AutoFit is a Word feature that automatically adjusts the column or row size to accommodate the longest texts in the table.

1. Select the row, column, or table you want to autofit.
2. Go to the **Table Tools Layout** tab.
3. Click the **AutoFit** drop-down button.
4. Select an option as desired from the menu.

48

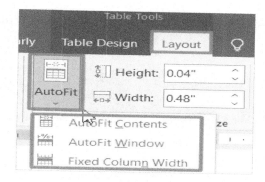

To adjust the column or row size using the Table Tools.

1. Click in the cell of the column you want to resize.
2. Select the **Layout** tab in the **Table Tools** contextual tab.
3. Set the width or height of column or row respectively as desired.

You can enter the desired number in the textbox directly or use the arrow up or down to increase or decrease the number.

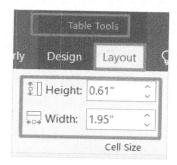

4.3.4 Merging Cells, Splitting cells, or Table.

Merging cells means combining two or more adjacent cells to form one cell, while splitting means dividing one cell into two or more.

To merge cells, split cells, or table:

1. Select the cells you want to merge/split or all the cells in the table boundary you want to split.
2. Go to **Layout** in the **Table Tools** contextual tabs.

3. Select either **Merge Cells, Split Cells, or Split Table** depending on wha you want to do.

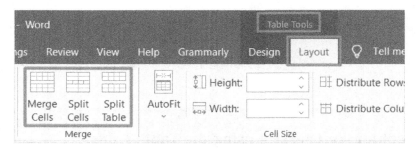

4.3.5 Repeating Table Headers across the Pages

If you have a very long table in your document that will run across many page of your document, for easy navigation, each pages the table runs should have it headers. Word table can be set up for this.

To set up the table to automatically repeat the header row(s) on each page:

1. Select the header row of the table.
2. Go to the contextual **Layout** ribbon in the **Table Tools** tab.
3. Click **Repeat Header Rows** in the **Data** group.

Alternatively,

1. Right-click within the table header.
   A drop-down menu appears.
2. Select **Table Properties**.
   Table Properties dialog box appears.
3. Click the **Row** tab.
4. Check **Repeat as header row at the top of each page** box.
5. Press **OK**.

4.3.6 Erasing Part of a Table

To erase a part of a table:

1. Click within your table.
2. Go to the **Layout** in the **Table Tools** tabs.
3. Select **Eraser**

    Your cursor turns to an eraser.
4. Move your cursor (now eraser) to the line you want to remove.
5. Drag your mouse on the line to erase it.

    Any line your eraser touches will be selected and erased when you release your mouse. Repeat as many lines as you want.
6. Press the **Esc** button on your keyboard when you are done.

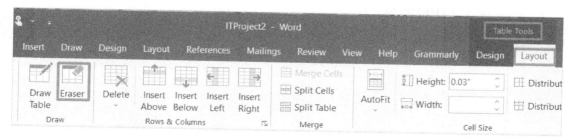

4.3.7 Deleting Cells, Rows, Columns, or Table

To delete cells, rows, columns, or a table:

1. Select the cell or cells you want to delete.
2. Go to the **Layout** in the **Table Tools** tab.
3. Click the **Delete** command.
   The **Delete** options appear.
4. Select the desired option based on what you want to do.

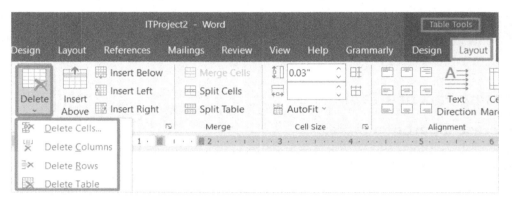

4.3.8 Table Borders

Word automatically puts a ½ inch border line around your table when inserted. You can remove/add and format any part of the borders following the steps below.

To remove, add and format borders:

1. Select the table.
2. Go to the **Home** tab.
3. Click the border icon dropdown button in the **Paragraph** group.

4. Select a desired option in the drop-down menu.

   For more options on table-border, select **Borders and Shading…**

   A dialog box appears.

5. Set the border styles, line styles, line weight, color as desired.

6. Press **OK** to apply the settings.

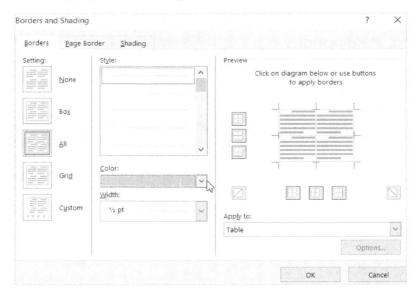

You can also access the border commands in the **Table Tools** contextual tab **Table Design**.

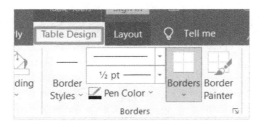

4.4 FORMATTING A TABLE

Word provides many features for you to format your table, as discussed below.

4.4.1 Applying Table Styles

For consistent formatting of the table and to save time, it is advisable to use table style.

To apply table style;

1. Position your cursor within the table.
2. Click the **Table Design** tab in the **Table Tools** contextual tab.
3. Select a style in the **Table Style** group or click the drop-down scroll bar for more style options.

   Your table style changes to the one your mouse is on, so you can hover over different ones to make your choice.

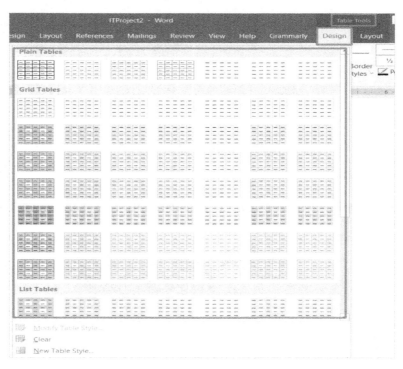

4.4.2 Table Style Options

Table Style Options are available for the unique styling of tables. They include:

- **Header Row**: This formats the first row of the table specially, if checked.
- **Total Row**: This provides an additional last row that gives information about the table columns when checked. It is especially useful for tables containing numbers as it gives the column's sum or average.
- **Banded Rows or Banded Columns**: It formats even and odd rows or columns differently if checked. This is good for easy visualization of the table.
- **First or Last Column**: This formats the first column or last column differently if checked.

To apply any of the table style options:

1. Place your cursor within the table.
2. Select **Table Design** in the **Table Tools** contextual tab.
3. Check and uncheck the options as desired.

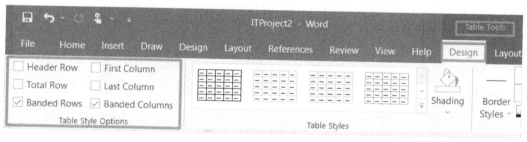

4.4.3 Modifying Table Styles and Styles Properties

You can modify your table style after applying it, and this modification will be applied to any table that uses the style.

To modify a table style and properties:

1. Place your cursor in the table.

2. Go to **Table Design** in the **Table Tools** tab.
3. Click on the scroll bar for more styles dialog box.
4. Select **Modify Table Style** or right-click on a table style and select **Modify.**

   A dialog box appears.
5. Modify as desired the **format**, i.e., font size, font style, font color, and the likes.
6. Click on the **Format** button to set further the style properties.

   Table properties dialog box appears.
7. Select the property you wish to set.

   A dialog box appears for you to make your settings.

   Press OK when done to close the properties dialog box.
8. Check the radio button:

   - **Only in this document** if you want the modification to be applied to only the current document.

   - **New Documents based on this template** if you want the modification to apply to future documents that apply the style.
9. Press **OK**.

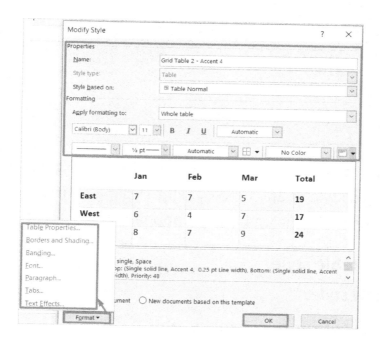

Note: It is important to note that a manually applied table formatting will override a table style.

4.4.4 Creating a New Table Style.

If you do not want to use or modify the built-in table styles, you can create your table style.

To create a custom table style:

1. Place your cursor within the table.
2. Select **Table Design** in the **Table Tools** tab.
3. Click the scroll bar for more styles dialog box.
4. Click **New Table Style**.
   A dialog box appears.
5. Name and format the style as desired.

The new table style appears at the top of the styles group under the **Custom**
You can delete the style at any time by right-clicking on it and selecting the **Delete**
Table Style option in the dialog box that appears.

4.4.5 Clearing a table style.

To clear a table style:

1. Place your cursor within the table.
2. Go to **Design** in the **Table Tools** tabs.
3. Click the down arrow in the **Style** group to open the more styles box.
4. Click on **Clear**.

Alternatively,

1. Right-click on the style.
   A dialog box appears.
2. Select the **Delete Table Style** option.

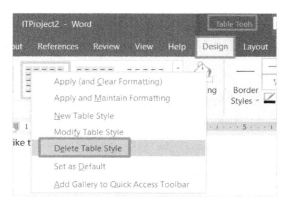

4.4.6 Setting a Default Table Style.

The default table style is the style of the new table inserted in your document.

To set your default table style:

1. Place your cursor within the table.
2. Go to **Table Design** in the **Table Tools** tabs.
3. Click the down arrow in the **Style** group to open the more styles box.
4. Right-click on the style you want as default.
5. Select **Set as Default** from the drop-down menu.
   A dialog box appears.
6. Select an option and click **OK**.

4.5 INSERTING FORMULAS IN TABLE

Word has a feature that allows you to use formulas and functions such as SUM, AVERAGE, MIN, MAX, and basic operators in your table to perform calculations. Each cell of the table is assigned a cell reference A1, A2... B1, B2, ... and so on. Columns are tagged alphabetically, and rows are numbered. A descriptive word such as **ABOVE**, **BELOW**, **LEFT** and **RIGHT** can also be used as arguments in the formulas.

To insert a formula in a table:

1. Click the cell you want to enter the formula.
2. Go to the table contextual **Layout** ribbon.
3. Click the **Function** command in the **Data** group.

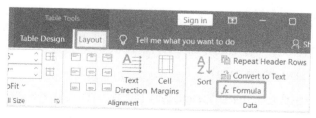

A dialog box appears with Word suggesting the likely formula you want.

4. Click **OK** to accept the suggested formula, or click in the **Formula** box and input your desired formula starting with = sign. You can also change the function in the **Paste Function** dropdown list.

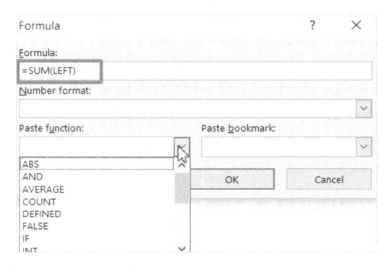

5. Select a format from the Format dropdown menu if necessary.
6. Click **OK** and Word insert the formula's result in the cell.

Word does not update your formula automatically in case you change your data.

To update a formula:

1. Select the formula cell or table.
2. Right-click and select **update** in the drop-down list that appears
   Or press **F9**.

To change a formula in a Table:

1. Select and right-click in the formula cell or error (if you get an error and need to edit the formula).
2. Select **Edit Field** in the dropdown menu that appears.

3. Make your desired changes.
4. Click **OK**.

4.6 CONVERTING TEXT TO TABLE AND VISE VERSA

Assuming you have a long list of text or numbers in your document and later decide to put it in a tabular form, Word has an amazing easy feature to do that with just a click and save you minutes of manual input.

To convert your text to table:

1. Select your text list.
2. Go to the **Home** tab.
3. Click the **Table** command
4. Select **Convert Text to Table** in the drop-down list.
   A dialog box appears.
5. Set the number of **columns** you want, and the number of rows automatically update to fit your data.
6. Check a **Separate text at** button based on what you separate the text with.
7. Click **OK** when you are done, and Word automatically converts your texts to a table.

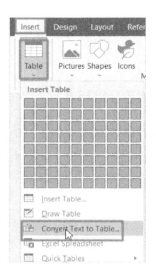 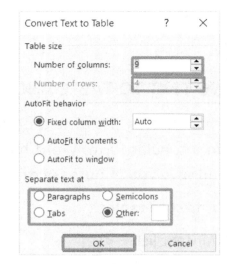

To convert a table to text:

1. Select the table.
2. Go to the Table Tools **Layout** ribbon.

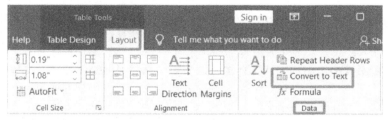

3. Click the **Convert to Text** button in the Data group.
   A dialog box appears.
4. Check the **Separate text with** options as desired.
5. Click OK, and Word automatically converts your table to text.

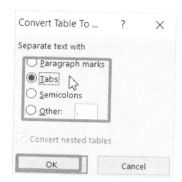

4.7 INSERTING A CHART INTO YOUR DOCUMENT

A chart is another Word feature that enables you to virtually present your information or data. You can insert any type of chart in your Word document.

To insert a chart in your document:

1. Place your insertion point where you want the chart.
2. Go to the **Insert** ribbon.
3. Click **Chart** in the **Illustration** group.
   Insert Chart dialog box appears.

4. Select a chart type and double Click on the desired chart.

    The chart appears in your document with an excel spreadsheet.

5. Input your data into the excel spreadsheet, and the charts update to your data.

6. Close the spreadsheet window.

4.8 FORMATTING A CHART.

1. Select the chart.
2. Click on the plus sign at the right top corner.
3. Check or uncheck the box of any elements to put or remove them from the chart.
4. Click on the arrow in front of any selected elements for more settings.
5. Click on **More Options...** to have control of the element from the element Format dialog box.

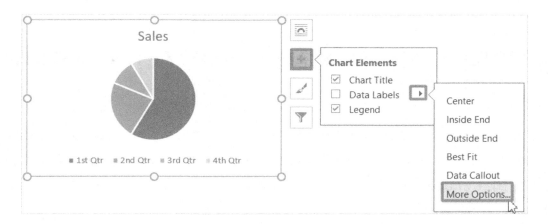

Each element has its **Format** dialog box to format your chart elements fully. You can change their color, width, size, gap, etc., from there as the case may be. The format dialog box can also be opened by:

- double-clicking on the element or
- Right-clicking on the element and choose **Format Data Series** from the list of the options or
- Using the keyboard shortcut command **Ctrl + 1** on the element.

You can also format your chart in the contextual **Chart Tools** tap (Design and Format buttons) or at the brush icon , the chart style below the **+** sign. You can filter your chart using the chart filter below the chart style icon.

CHAPTER 5: IMAGES, SHAPES, SMARTART, AND TEXTBOX

While working on your document, there are times you need to illustrate your work with shapes, pictures, or images and a movable textbox. Word provides features that enable you to do that without stress. Below are step-by-step guides on how to work with illustrations in your document.

5.1 INSERTING IMAGES

To add an image to your document:

1. Place your cursor where you want your picture to be.
2. Go to the **Insert** ribbon.
3. Click the **Picture** command in the **Illustration** group.
   The **Insert Picture From** menu box appears.
4. a. Select **This Device**... if your image is on your computer.
      An **Insert Picture** dialog box appears.
   b. Select **Online Pictures...** if you want to use an online image.
      Your default browser opens.
5. a. Select and open the image folder. Frow the left menu, you can open another location to search for the image. Select your image.
   b. Browse for your desired image.
6. Click the **Insert** button or double-click on the image.

Alternatively, you can copy the image wherever it is and paste it into you document.

5.2 INSERTING SCREENSHOTS

You can insert screenshots of any opened window on your system in your document.

To capture and insert a screenshot in your document:

1. Place your mouse where you want your screenshot to be.
2. Open and display the image or document you want to capture on your computer screen.
3. Click on the **Insert** tab.
4. Select **Screenshot** in the **Illustration** group.
   A drop-down menu appears, showing you the available whole window screenshots.
5. a. Select the desired available screenshot if you want to capture the whole screen, and Word automatically inserts the screenshot in your document.

   b. Select **Screen Clipping** to capture a part of any of the windows.
      Your cursor turns to a plus icon, and your screen turns blurred.
6. Click, hold, and drag the mouse to select your desired portion of the window.
7. Release your hand when done, and Word automatically inserts your selected portion of the window into your document.

NOTE: To insert your desktop screenshot, close or minimize all documents that can interfere with the screen. You do not need to close the document you are working with for Word closes it automatically when you select **Screen Clipping** as you follow the above steps.

5.3 INSERTING SHAPES.

Different shapes like circles, rectangles, lines, arrows and more, are available i Word for your use.

To add shapes to your document:

1. Click the **Insert** tab.
2. Select the **Shapes** command in the **Illustrations** group.
   The Shapes dialog box appears with all the available shapes.
3. Click on any of the shapes as desired.
   Your cursor turns to a cross.
4. Move to the location in your document where you want your shape t be.
5. Click and drag to draw the shape to the desired size.

Tips: The shape turns itself off after each use, to keep it active for continuous use

- Select and right-click on it
- Select **Lock Drawing Mode** from the menu that appears.
- Draw the shape as many times as desired.
- Press the **Esc** key or click on the shape icon again when you are done.

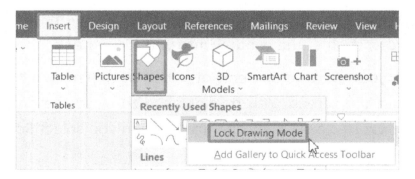

You can as well add text to your shape.

To add text to your shape:

1. Click inside the shape.
2. Type in your text.

Format your text just like any other text in your document as desired.

5.4 ADDING SMARTART TO YOUR DOCUMENT.

SmartArt visually communicates essential ideas, information, and processes with graphical presentation.

Word has a gallery of SmartArt that consists of a list, process, cycle, hierarchy, etc., to meet your specific requirement.

To add a SmartArt to your document:

1. Place the insertion point where you want your SmartArt.
2. Go to **Insert** ribbon.
3. Click on **SmartArt** in the **Illustration** group.
   A dialog box appears.

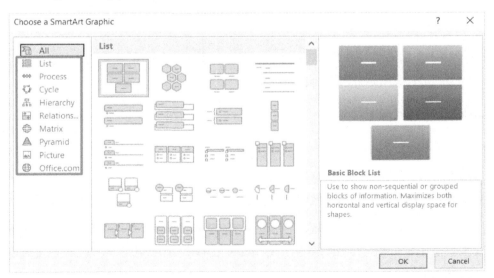

4. Click on the SmartArt type that best describes what you want to do, e.g., list, process, cycle, etc.

5. Select one of the SmartArt type varieties as desired.
6. Press **OK,** and Word inserts the SmartArt with a pane.
7. Replace the **SmartArt** pane text with your texts.
   For more items, press **Enter** in the last item, and Word automaticall
   creates more places for you to continue.

With the SmartArt is a contextual **Design** and **Format** tabs for you to format you
SmartArt.

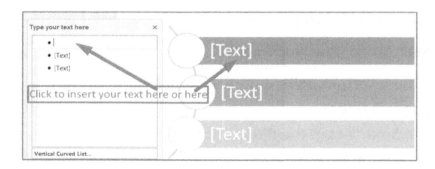

Designing SmartArt

Various options are available to set up, organize and design your SmartArt t
your taste after you have inserted it.

To design your SmartArt:

1. Select the SmartArt.
2. Go to the contextual **SmartArt Design** tab.
3. Make the desired changes:
   - Click on **Change Color** or the **SmartArt Styles** gallery drop-down arrow
     to see the list of different colors template you can select and apply t
     your SmartArt.

- To rearrange your points in the SmartArt, select the shape and click the **Move Up** or **Move Down** commands in the **Create Graphic** group.
- To change the list level of a selected shape or bullet, click the **Promote**, or **Demote** command in the **Create Graphic** group.
- You can change the SmartArt layout from left to right and vice visa by selecting or deselecting the **Right to Left** command.
- If you need more than the three available shapes, click the **Add Shape** button in the **Create Graphic** group to add more shapes.
- If you need more than the available bullet on the shape, click the **Add Bullet** button in the **Create Graphic** group to add more bullets.
- You can hide or Unhide the text pane on your slide by clicking the **Text Pane** button in the **Create Graphic** group.
- You can convert your SmartArt to text or shapes by clicking the **Convert** drop-down arrow and selecting the desired option.
- If your SmartArt has picture icons, click on the icon, and follow the prompt to add your desired picture.
- Click the **Reset Graphic** button to undo all the settings if you wish to.

5.5 WORKING WITH TEXTBOX

A textbox is an object that allows you to type your text and place it anywhere in your document. Using a textbox makes working with text flexible.

To insert a textbox:

1. Click **Insert** tab.

2. Select **Text box** in the **Text** group.
   A dialog box appears with preformatted textbox options.
3. Select an option as desired, and textbox appears in your document or
   -Select **More Text Box from Office.com** to get more text box options or
   the Microsoft Office website.
   Select **Draw Text Box** if you wish to draw your text box to your desired
   size manually. Your cursor turns to a cross.
   - Click the point you want to put your textbox and drag to draw to
     your desired size.
4. Type in your text and click anywhere outside the box when you are done

To Edit your text box:

1. Double click on the text box and edit like the normal word document.
2. Use your arrow keys to navigate in the textbox.

5.6 WORKING WITH WORDART

A WordArt is a form of a textbox with additional styles. Word has a gallery of
WordArt with different styles that you can quickly apply to your texts to change
their appearance and styles.

To use WordArt in your document:

1. Click on the **Insert** tab.
2. Select **WordArt** in the **Text** group.
   WordArt drop-down menu appears.
3. Click on the desired style, and it appeared in your document as a text box
   with the text format as the style of letter **A** in the gallery.
4. Type in your text and click anywhere outside the box when you are done

To Edit your text box:

1. Double click on the text box and edit like the normal word document.
2. Use your arrow keys to navigate in the textbox.

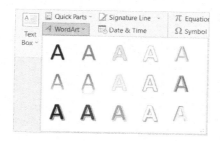

5.7 OBJECT LAYOUT (MAKE OBJECT FLOATS WITH TEXT WRAPPING)

Word inserts an object **in line** with text by default, but different options are available to change the object layout relative to the text. Using any of the **With Text Wrapping** options makes your object float, i.e., you can select and move it freely to any location, whether there is text or no text in the place. It also allows you to write on your image.

To make your object float:

1. Select the object.
2. Click the **Layout Options** icon, ⬚ that appears at the top right side of the object, or Go to the contextual **Format** ribbon and select **Wrap Text.**

   A drop-down menu appears.
3. Select an option in the **With Text Wrapping** option depending on how you want your image to relate to the text.

Hover on each option to see their names and how the layout works with text with the icon. For example, this icon ![icon] called **Behind Text** shows that the object will be at the back of the text if it is moved to where there is text.

There are also two options for you to either move the object with text or fix the object's position on-page. Check any of the desired options.

For more layout, select **See more**.

5.8 FORMATTING AND EDITING OBJECTS

Objects are shape, picture, image, screenshot, WordArt, Textbox, and SmartArt. When selected, any of the objects will have a contextual object **Format** tab that can be used to format the object. Most of the Format commands are the same across all the objects, and most of them are for visual effects enhancement of the object.

5.8.1 Selecting an Object

To format an object, the first thing you do is to select the object. Follow the steps below to select an object:

- Click inside of the object.

- Move your cursor to any part of the object outline. Your cursor turns to four-headed arrows.
- Click on the outline.

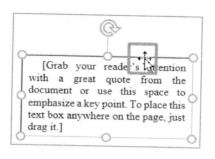

5.8.2 Deleting an Object

1. Select the image you want to delete.
   Selection handles appear around the image.
2. Press Delete or Backspace button on your keyboard, and your image is removed.

5.8.3 Applying Visual Effects Enhancement to an Object

MS Word has impressive features that you can use to make changes to your object after you have inserted it into your document. You can make the following changes with Word features.

For Picture and some other objects:

- **Corrections:** It adjusts your image brightness, contrast, sharpness, or softness in different proportions.
- **Color:** It changes the color of your image with different shades from color to black and white.
- **Artistic Effects:** It changes your image to look like a sketch or paint of different styles.
- **Compress Pictures:** It reduces the size of your image.

- **Change Picture:** It makes you change your picture to another one retaining the size and format of your current picture.
- **Reset Picture:** To undo all the changes you have made to the image.
- **Picture Border:** It helps to put an outline around the image, and the outline color, width, and style can be changed as desired.
- **Picture Effects:** It applies effects like shadow, reflection, glows, etc., to your image.
- **Picture Layout:** It makes your image easy to edit by converting it to a SmartArt graphic.

Other formatting features for most objects include:

- **Object Fill** : Selecting this command fills your shape with the default or last applied color. Click on the drop-down button to select a desired fill color in the color palette.
- **Object Outline** : Selecting this command, put borders around your object with the default or last applied color. Click on the drop-down button to select a desired outline color in the color palette.
- **Object Effect** : This gives your object some artistic effects like shadow, reflection, glow, 3-D rotation, and so on. Click on the command, select from the effects option, and choose a desired version of the effects.
- **Object Style:** This contains a gallery of preformatted objects for you quick use.

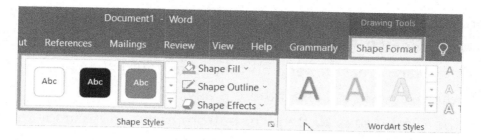

To make changes to your object using any of the features above:

1. Select the object.
    The object **Format** contextual tab appears.
2. Click the object **Format** tab.
3. Select the effect you want to apply, e.g., **Corrections, Border, Artistic Effects, fill, etc.**
4. If the effect has a drop-down icon, click on it, and select an option as desired.

The object style in the **Format** ribbon depends on the type of object you inserted.

5.8.4 Remove Picture Background with MS Word

Word has a feature that can help you remove the background of your picture for quick use.

To remove an image background:

1. Select the picture or image. Picture Format tab appears.
2. Go to the **Picture Format** tab

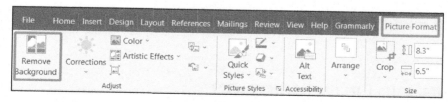

3. Select **Remove Background** command.

Word changes the color of the background it wants to remove and open the **Background Removal** ribbon for you to make an adjustment.

4. Click the **Mark Areas to Keep** button, go to your image and mark out some part you would like to keep if there is any.
5. Click the **Mark Areas to Remove** button, move your cursor to your image and mark out some part you wish to remove but was not highlighted, if any.
6. Select **Keep Changes** to remove the background when you are done or
7. Select **Discard All Changes** to keep the picture's background.

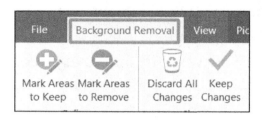

5.8.5 Writing on an Image/Picture.

To write on an image:

1. Insert your image.
2. Change your image layout to **Behind Text** in the **With Text Wrapping** option.
3. Insert a textbox or WordArt and format as desired.
4. Move your text on top of the image.
5. Select the Image and the textbox or WordArt.
6. Group them together.

Note: Consult other sections of this chapter on how to insert, text wrapping, and group objects.

5.9 RESIZING AND CROPPING OBJECT

To resize your image:

1. Select the image you want to resize.

   Handle borders appear around the image.

2. Click and drag on any of the handles as desired.

   The image changes size as you drag to the left, right, up, or down.

3. Release your mouse when the size of the image is as desired.

Note: Use the corner handles for uniform increase/decrease in your image size.

Alternatively,

1. Select the object.
2. Go to the contextual **Format** tab.
3. Enter the actual height and width in the text boxes provided (or use the arrows) in the **Size** group.

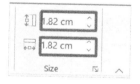

Cropping

Cropping an image allows you to remove some outer parts of an image.

To crop an image:

1. Click the image you want to crop.
2. Go to the object **Format** tab.
3. Click the **Crop** button in the Size group.

Crop handle appears around the image borders

4. -Drag the **side cropping handle** inside to crop the side

   - Drag the **corner cropping handle** inside to crop two adjacent sides equally and simultaneously.

   - To crop two parallel sides at the same time, press and hold down the **Ctrl** key as you drag the side cropping handle simultaneously.

5. Press **Esc** on your keyboard when you are done.

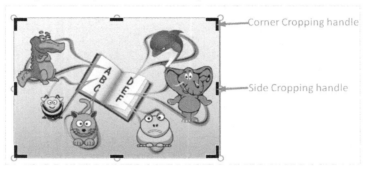

For more cropping options, click on the **Crop** command drop-down icon and select an option from the menu.

- The **Crop to Shape** allows you to crop your image to the desired shape from the list that appears.

- **Aspect Ratio** gives you some ratio at which you can crop your work.

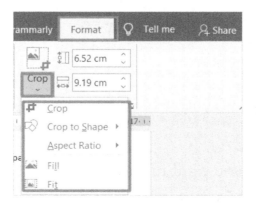

Can you try something like this?

Change  **to**

5.10 MOVING, ROTATING AND FLIPPING IMAGE

To move your image from a place to the other:

1. Select the image.
   Handle borders appear around the image.
2. Click, hold down, and drag the image to the desired location.

To copy, cut, and paste an object

1. Click the object to select it.
   The object border appears.
2. Click the border of the object
   -Press **Ctrl + C** to copy or **Ctrl + X** to cut

Alternatively,

-Right-click on the border. A dialog box appears.

-Select **Cut** or **Copy** as desired.

3. Place your cursor where you want the text box to be
4. Press **Ctrl + V** to paste the text box.

To rotate your image:

1. Click the image you want to rotate.
   Handle borders appear around the image.
2. Select the rotating handle at the top of the image.

Your cursor turns to a circular arrow.

3. Rotate the image clockwise or anticlockwise as desired.

Alternatively, and in other to **flip** the image:

1. Select the image you want to rotate/flip.
2. Go to the **Picture Format** tab.
3. Click the **Rotate** command in the **Arrange** group.
   A drop-down menu appears.
4. Select an option.

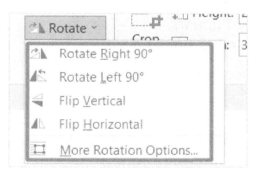

5.11 ALIGNING, ORDERING, AND GROUPING OBJECTS IN WORD

Suppose you will be working with multiple objects like images/pictures, shapes, textbox, and WordArt in your document. In that case, it is essential to know how to align, order, and group objects appropriately.

NOTE: To align, order, or group objects, you need to select them, and for you to be able to select multiple objects in Word, you must ensure that their layout is any of the **With Text Wrapping** options (See **section 5.12** to do that).

5.11.1 Aligning Objects

To align two or more objects:

1. Hold down the **Ctrl** or **Shift** key and click on the individual objects you want to align to select them.
2. Click on the **object Format** tab
3. Select **Align** command in the **Arrange** group. Align drop-down options appear.
4. Word aligns the objects in their current position by default. To align with page or margin, select an option in the 3rd group as shown above.
5. Select one of the alignment options as desired.

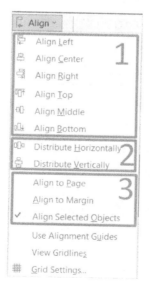

Note: The alignment options in the 1st and 2nd groups are relative to the 3rd group options.

You can use the second group to **equally** distribute your objects horizontally or vertically in relation to the 3rd group.

5.11.2 Ordering Objects

Ordering an object is important when two or more objects will have to overlap. Objects are placed on top of one another according to the order in which you inserted them into your document, creating different **levels**. Ordering the objects means changing their levels as desired.

To change an object's level:

1. Select the object you want to change its level.
2. Click the **Format** tab.
3. Click the **Send Backward** or **Bring Forward** drop-down in the **Arrange** group.
   A drop-down menu appears.
4. Select an option, and Word automatically reorders your object.
   - **Send Backward** and **Bring Forward** send your object one level backward and forward, respectively.
   - **Send to Back and Bring to Front** sends your object behind and in front of all objects, respectively.
   - **Send Behind Text and Bring in Front of Text** makes the text and image feasible, respectively.

Alternatively, to have more control over your ordering,

3. Select the **Selection Pane** command in the Arrange group.
   The selection navigation pane appears at the right side of your window with the list of all the objects starting from the first object at the top to the last object at the back.

4. To rearrange; Select, Drag and Drop any object to the desired level.

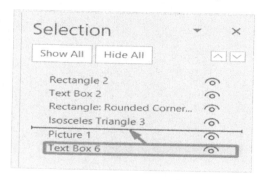

5.11.3 Grouping or Ungrouping Objects

You may sometimes want some of your objects to stay together when working on your document. This can be achieved by grouping.

To group objects:

1. Select your objects by holding the **Ctrl** or **Shift** key and clicking on the individual objects.

2. Click on the **Format** tab.

3. Select **Group** in the **Resize** group.

Then your objects will now be a singular object that can be moved, resized, and formatted together like one.

To Ungroup your objects:

1. Select the grouped object.

2. Click on the **Format** tab.

3. Select the **Group** command drop-down icon.

4. Select **Ungroup** from the menu that appear

CHAPTER 6: FONT AND PARAGRAPH FORMATTING

Formatting in Word can be categorized into four:

- **<u>Font or character Formatting</u>**: This allows you to format text with **Font type**, **Font size**, **Color**, **Highlight**, and **Text effect**.
- **<u>Paragraph Formatting</u>:** This includes **Text alignment, Line spacing, Tabs, Indents, Bullet** and **Numbering, Borders,** and **Shades.**
- **<u>Page or Document Formatting</u>**: This includes **Margins, Page size, Page orientation, Headers and Footers, Page Numbering,** etc.
- **<u>Section Formatting</u>:** This requires **Page Breaks** and **Section Breaks.**

Knowing about these four formatting types will save you time and make your document formatting less frustrating.

6.1 FONT FORMATTING

Font formatting changes the appearance of a group of words or characters individually. Most of the commands used for font formatting are available in the **Home** ribbon in the **Font** group. Additional commands can be explored by clicking the dialog box launcher ⌧ .

To format text:

1. Select the text you want to format.
2. Go to the **Home** ribbon.
3. Select as desired:
   - **Font type** dropdown list to change the shape of the text.

- **Number** dropdown `14 ▾` list or the **Increase and Decrease** buttons `A A` to change the text font size.
- **Bold** `B` to make the text darker and thicker.
- *Italics* `I` to slant the text.
- <u>Underline</u> `U ▾` to underline the text with a single black line. Click the dropdown button in the front to choose the underline color and style.
- ~~Strikethrough~~ `abc` to draw a line through the text.
- Subscript `x₂` to make the text small below the text line usually used for chemical formulas, e.g., H_2O.
- Superscript `x²` to make the text slightly above the line of text.
- Text Effects `A ▾` dropdown lists to apply different effects styles to the text.
- Font Color `A ▾` to change the color of the text. The color you selected last will be applied to your text. To change the color, use the dropdown icon.
- **Text Highlight Color** `ab ▾` to change the text background color.
- `A` to clear all the text formatting.
- **Change Case** `Aa ▾` to choose from one of its five options:
    o **Sentence case** capitalizes only the first letter.
    o **lowercase** put all the text in lower letters.
    o **UPPERCASE** capitalizes all the letters of the text
    o **Capitalize Each Word** capitalizes only the first letter of each word of the text, and
    o **tOGGLE cASE** put only the first letter in lower case and all others in uppercase.

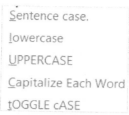

Sentence case.

lowercase

UPPERCASE

Capitalize Each Word

tOGGLE cASE

4. For more options, click the dialog box launcher.

A **Font** dialog box appears.

5. Click the **Advance** tab to change letters width relative to height, spacing, text or object position, and any other desired settings.

(The effects of **S p a c i n g** and **Position** settings are illustrated with the words. The spacing can even be set so that the letters overlap. The position can also be lowered instead of raised.)

6. Press **OK** when you are done with the settings.

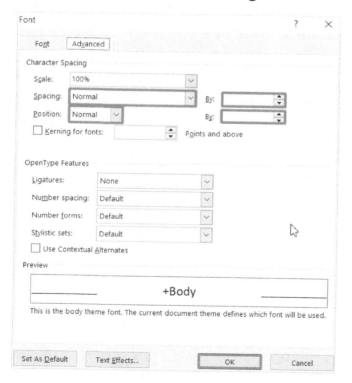

6.2 SETTING LINE SPACING

Line spacing is the vertical distance between lines. Setting line spacing affect the paragraph where the cursor is positioned or all the selected paragraphs.

To set your document line spacing

1. Select the entire document.
2. Click the **Home** tab
3. Click the line spacing icon in the **Paragraph** group.
   A drop-down list appears.
4. Select your desired number spacing.

Word effects the spacing as you hover over the numbers. Before choosing, yo can check how it all looks if you do not have a number in mind.

To set the line spacing of a paragraph, position your cursor anywhere in th paragraph and follow the steps above.

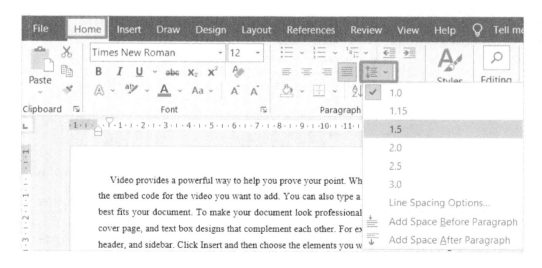

6.3 TEXT ALIGNMENT

Text alignment is a formatting attribute that determines the appearance and location of texts in a whole paragraph with respect to the margin. There are four main text alignments in Word, namely:

- **Left alignment:** It aligns your paragraph to the left margin.

- **Center alignment**: It aligns your paragraph at the center of the page.

- **Right alignment**: It aligns your paragraph to the right margin.

- **Justified**: It aligns your document to the right and left margins and adds extra spaces where necessary except for the last line.

Left alignment is the Word's default alignment, and it is appropriate for most situations. You can use center alignment for headings, right alignment for a date, and justified if you want a smooth look of your document edges.

To align your document:

1. Select the whole document or the paragraph you want to align.
2. Go to the **Home** tab.
3. Click on any of the desired alignment commands in the **Paragraph** group.

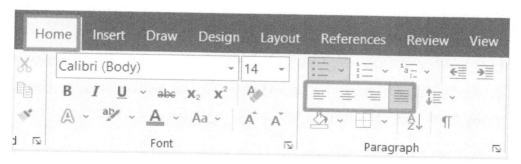

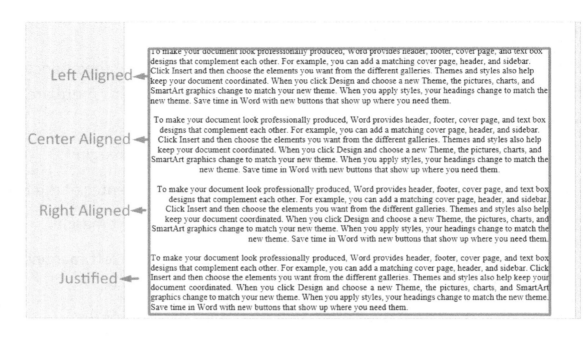

6.4 INDENTATION

Indentation is used for shifting the edge of a paragraph or line inward or outward, as the case may be.

There are four available types of Indentation in Word, namely:

- **First-line indent**: In this case, only the first line of the paragraph or section is shifted inside or outside the center of the page.
- **Hanging indent**: All other lines except the first line of the paragraph or section are indented.
- **Left indent:** All the lines in the paragraph are indented in relation to the document's left margin, i.e., the lines are shifted inside the page and away from the left margin for positive value and otherwise for a negative value.
- **Right indent:** All the lines in the paragraph are indented in relation to the right margin of the document, i.e., the lines are shifted inside the page

and away from the right margin for positive value and otherwise for a negative value.

The **Left indent** command button is available in the **Home** tab in the **Paragraph** group as two buttons to:

- **Increase Indent** and
- **Decrease Indent**

These buttons decrease or increase the indent by **5"** per click. If you want to set a desired indent, go to the **Layout** tab, and under Paragraph group, input your indent.

First-Line indent and **hanging indent** are special indents that can be set by opening the dialog box launcher in the Paragraph group.

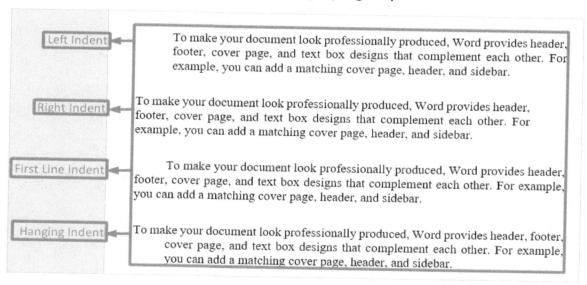

To add indent to a paragraph:

1. Place your cursor anywhere in the paragraph or highlight the section you want to add indent.
2. Go to the **Home** or **Layout** tab.

3. Click the dialog box launcher in the **Paragraph** group.

   A **Paragraph** dialog box appears.

4. Set your **Left** or **Right** indent under **Indentation**.

5. Click the drop-down button under **Special** to select either **First line** o

   Hanging depending on what you want, set the value under **By**.

   You can preview the indented effect under **Preview**.

6. Click **OK.**

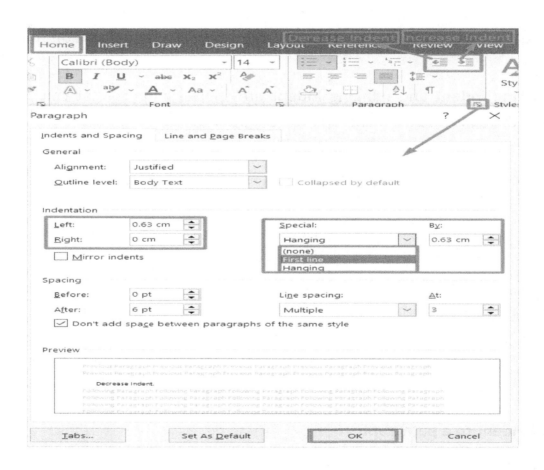

6.5 FORMATTING LISTS INDENT

You can format your list indent to change the position of the bullets/numberings in a list or the space between the text and the bullets/numberings.

To change your lists, indent:

1. Select the bullets/numbering by clicking on one of the bullets/numbers.
2. Right-click on the selected bullets.
   A dialog box appears.
3. Select **Adjust List Indents;** its dialog box appears.
4. Set the **Bullet position box** to change the distance of the bullet or numbering indent from the margin.
5. Set **Text indent** box to change the distance between the texts and the bullets or numbering.
6. Select either **Tab character, Space,** or **Nothing** in the **Follow number with** box.
7. Click **OK** when you are done with your settings.
   Word effects the changes.

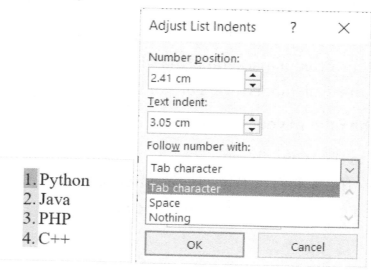

To change the indent of only one bullet or numbering:

1. Click next to the text of the bullet you want to modify.
2. Go to the **Home** tab and in the **Paragraph** group.
3. Select the **Multilevel list** arrow.
   A dialog box appears.
4. Select **Change List Level.**
5. Select the level you want in the dialog box that appears.

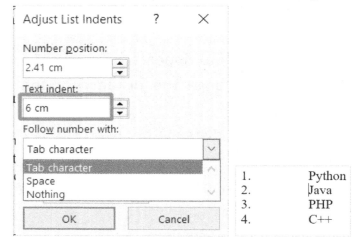

6.6 USING THE RULER IN MS WORD

Rulers in Word are provided to make working on your document layout easy. It is used to control your paragraph margin, indents, and tab stops. This feature works the same in all modern versions of Word from Word 2010 till 2019.

To view the ruler in your document in case it is hidden:

- Go to the **View** ribbon.
- Click the **Ruler** checkbox in the **Show** group to mark it.
  Then the rulers show on your document.

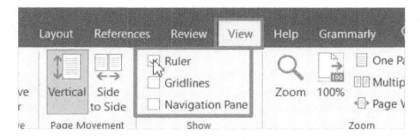

Given below are the various items on the horizontal ruler:

- **First Line Indent**
- **Hanging Indent**
- **Left Indent**
- **Right Indent**
- **Tab Stop**

The ruler's items show the cursor's current paragraph indentation.

Instead of setting your paragraph indentations as discussed in **section 6.4**, you can make use of the ruler.

To use a ruler to set your Paragraph indentations:

1. Select the text/paragraph you want to set the indent or Position your cursor anywhere in the paragraph.
2. Move your cursor to the horizontal ruler.
3. Click and drag the desired indent item to the right or left as desired.

Tab Control

Using the **Tab** key on the keyboard gives you control to place your text in the desired position on a line. By default, pressing the Tab key moves your insertion point ½ inch to the right. The size of the tabs can be changed by using the ta[b] stops, and you can add more than one on a line.

To the left of the ruler is the tab stop selector showing the active tab stop typ[e]. Click on the tab stop selector repeatedly to see the different types. Listed belo[w] are types of the tab stop.

- **Left tab stop** ⌞ : It left aligns your text at the tab stop position.

- **Center tab stop** ⊤ : It centers your text around the tab stop position.

- **Right tab stop** ⌐ : It right aligns your text at the tab stop position.

- **Decimal tab stop** ⊤ : It aligns the decimal points of the decimal number.

- **Bar tab stop** ▯ : It draws a vertical line on your document.

- **First Line Indent** ▽ and **Hanging Indent** △ are the same as the indents o[f]

  the ruler.

To set a tab stop using the ruler:

1. Move your cursor to the tab stop selector.
2. Click on it continuously to select your desired tab control.
   Once your desired tab control shows.
3. Click the bottom of the horizontal ruler where you want your tab stop.
4. Place your insertion point in front of the text you want to tab.
5. Press the **Tab** key: Your text will jump to the next tab stop.

To clear the tab stop: Select and drag the tab stop down off the ruler.

6.7 FORMAT PAINTER

When you want to format a section of your document just like you have formatted one, instead of going through the stress of doing the formatting all over again, Word has a special command called **Format Painter** just for that. **Format Painter** copies the format of one and applies it to the other.

To use a Format Painter:

1. Select the text that has your desired format.
2. Go to the **Home** tab and in the **Clipboard** group.
3. Click once on the **Format Painter**.
   Your cursor turns to a paintbrush.
4. Move your cursor to the text you want to format.
5. Select the text.
   Word automatically formats the text like the one you copied.

Format Painter turns itself off after each use. To keep it active for continuous use,

- double-click on it.
- Press the **Esc** key or click on the icon again when you are done.

6.8 ADD A DROP CAP TO YOUR PARAGRAPH.

A drop cap is a short form of dropped capital, and this is a large capital letter used as **a decorative element** at the beginning of any section or paragraph. The drop cap letter-size usually spans two to more lines of the paragraph or section.

To add a Drop Cap to your paragraph or section:

1. Select the first letter of the paragraph/section you want to add drop cap.
2. Go to the **Insert** tab.
3. Click on **the Drop cap** command in the **Text** group.
   A drop-down menu appears.

4. Select your preferred option.

   Select **Drop Cap Options** to format the drop cap.

5. Select **Position**, **Font**, **Lines to drop,** and **Distance from text** as desired.
6. Press **OK**.

To remove a drop cap:

1. Select the drop cap letter.
2. Go to **the Insert** tab.
3. Click **Drop Cap** in the **Text** group.

   A drop menu appears.
4. Select **None.**

CHAPTER 7: DOCUMENT FORMATTING

7.1 FORMATTING WITH STYLES AND THEMES

Styles and **themes** are powerful Word features that you can quickly and easily use to create a professional-looking document. A **style** is a Word predefined combination of all font, and paragraph formatting elements (e.g., font size, font type, color, indent, etc.) applied to a selected text or paragraph. At the same time, a **theme** is a group of formatting choices with a unique set of colors, font, and effects to change the appearance of the entire document.

Word has a gallery of styles and themes for your use. Given below are how to apply, modify and create styles and themes.

7.1.1 Applying, Modifying, and Creating Styles

To apply a style:

1. Select the text or paragraph you want to apply a style.
2. Go to the **Home** ribbon.
3. Select the style you want in the **Style** group. You can hover over each style to see the live effect in your document before applying. To see the additional style, click the **More** dropdown arrow.

To modify a style:

1. Select the style you want to modify.

2. Right-click and select Modify in the dropdown list.

   A **Modify Style** dialog box appears.

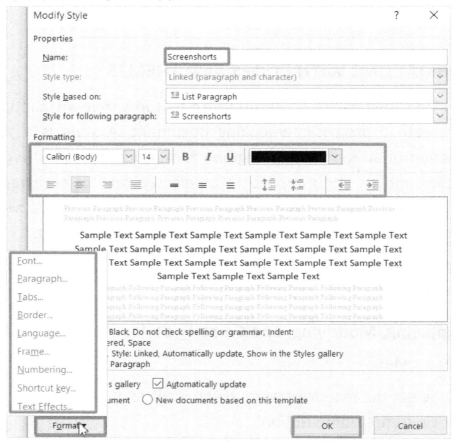

3. Set as desired all the formatting groups. You can as well change the style name.

4. Click on the **Format** button for more formatting options and control.

5. Check the **Automatically update** box to update the styles change anywhere you have applied them in your document.

6. Press **OK** when you are done.

To create a style:

1. Go to the **Home** ribbon.

2. In the **Style** group, click the **More** dropdown arrow.
3. Select **Create a Style**.

   A dialog box appears.
4. Input your desired name.
5. Click the **Modify** button, modify as explained above, and a new style will appear in the style gallery.

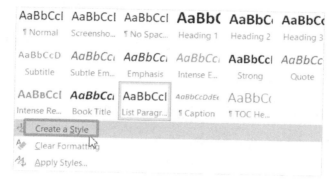

To remove a style from the list, right-click on the style and select **Remove from Style Gallery.**

7.1.2 Creating your Document with Word Headings

To create your document with Word Headings:

- Go to the **Home** ribbon, under **Style** group.
- Select all your chapters or section headings and click **Heading 1** in the **Style** group.
- Select all the sub-topics or sub-sections and click **Heading 2** in the **Style** group.
- Select all your sub-sub-topics and click **Heading 3** in the **Style** group. Continue to your last headings.

You can customize your headings following the steps in **Section 7.1.1**

7.1.3 Changing, Customizing, and Saving a Theme

A Theme is a set of fonts, colors, and effects that change the entire look of your document. Whenever you create a document in Word, you use the default **Office** theme.

To change the theme of your document:

1. Click the **Design** tab.

2. Click the **Themes** command in the **Document Formatting** group.

   A drop-down list appears.

3. Hover your cursor over a theme to preview it in your document.

4. Click your desired theme to apply it.

Customizing a theme

You can change any theme element (i.e., color, font, and effect) to create a unique look for your document.

To change themes colors:

1. Go to the **Design** tap.

2. Select **Colors** command.

   A drop-down color palette appears.

3. Select the desired color palate or click customize color to combine your colors.

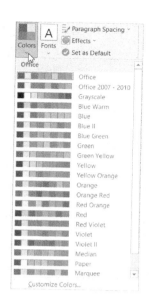

To change a theme font:

1. Go to the **Design** tab.

2. Click the **Font** command.

   A drop-down menu of fonts appears.

3. Select your desired theme fonts or

   Select **Customize Font** to customize your font. Set your desired font in the dialog box that appears and press **Ok**.

To change a theme effect:

1. Go to the **Design** tab.
2. Click the **Effect** command.
   A drop-down list of all the available effects appears.
3. Select the desired effect. You can see the live preview of any effect you hover on.

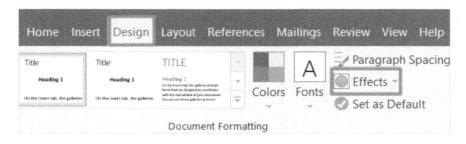

You can save your current or customized theme for later use.

To save a theme:

1. Click the **Design** tab.

2. Click the **Themes** command in the **Document Formatting** group.

   A drop-down list appears.

3. Select **Save Current Theme**.

4. Input a file name for your theme and press **Save** in the dialog box tha
   appears.

7.2 SETTING PAPER SIZE, MARGINS, AND ORIENTATION

Margins are the spaces between the edges of your document (top, bottom
left, and right) and your text. They make your work look professional. The defaul
margin in Word is 1 inch for all sides. There are predefined margins, and you can
as well customize your margins.

To apply a predefined margin to your document:

1. Go to the **Layout** ribbon.
2. Click on **Margins** in the **Page Setup** group.
   A drop-down menu appears.
3. Select an option from the list.

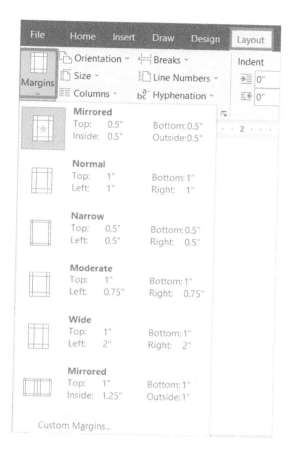

To customize your margin:

3. Select **Custom Margins...**
   A dialog box appears.
4. Input your values in the textboxes,
5. Select an option in **Apply to:** box.
6. Click **Set As Default** (optional)
7. Press **OK.**

   Note: Select the whole document first before applying a predefined margin to a document with different sections because Word applies the predefined margin only to the current section.

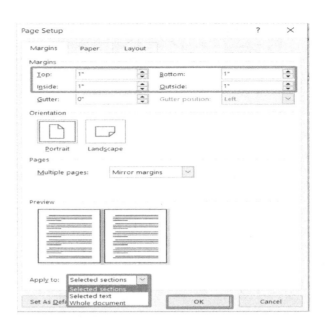

PAGE SIZE

To set Page Size:

1. Go to the **Layout** ribbon.
2. Click the **Size** button.

   A drop-down menu appears.
3. Select an option from the list.

To customize your page size:

3. Select **More Paper Sizes...**

   A dialog box appears.
4. Input your values in the Width and Height text boxes.
5. Select an option in **Apply to:** box.
6. Click **Set As Default** if you wish to set the size as default.
7. Press **OK**.

PAGE ORIENTATION:

To change your page orientation:

1. Go to the **Layout** ribbon.

2. Click the **Orientation** command.

   A drop-down menu appears.

3. Select **Portrait** for a vertical page or **Landscape** for a horizontal page.

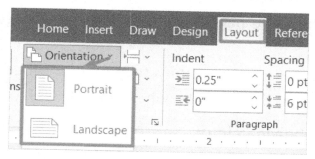

7.3 PAGE BREAKS AND SECTION BREAKS

When working on a document with multiple pages and many headings, it is sometimes challenging to format the document in such a way that all chapter headings start on a new page without some beginning at the bottom of a page. Also, when working on some types of documents with multiple sections like an article, report, paper, or book, it might be difficult to add **different** headers, footers, footnotes, page numbers, and other formatting elements.

Word duplicates the same headers, footers, footnotes and continues numbering throughout the entire document. To have a separate one, document **breaks** are required.

There are two types of documents breaks in Word:

- Page breaks
- Section breaks.

Page breaks partition the document's body while section breaks partition not only the document body but also the headings (or chapters), headers, footers, footnotes, page numbers, margins, etc.

Page Breaks are subdivided into:

- **Page break**: This forces all the text behind the insertion point to the next page
- **Column** break: This forces the text to the right of the insertion point to the next column of the same page when working with a document with multiple columns
- **Text Wrapping break**: It moves any text to the right of the cursor to the following line, and it is instrumental when working with objects.

Section Breaks are subdivided into:

- **Next Page break:** This divides the documents by creating another page that can have its special formatting. This is very useful for partitioning your document into different chapters with different headers, footers, page numbers, etc.
- **Continuous break:** This divides the document into sections that can be independently formatted on the same page without creating a new page. This type of break is usually used to change the number of columns on a page.
- **Even Page break:** This shifts the insertion point and any text at its right to the next even page.
- **Odd Page break**: This shifts the insertion point and any text at its right to the next odd page.

To Insert a Page Break or Section Break:

1. Place your insertion point to where you want the break.
2. Go to the **Layout** ribbon.
3. Select **Breaks** in the **Page Setup** group.
   A drop-down list appears with all the types of breaks.
4. Select from the options the type of section break you want.

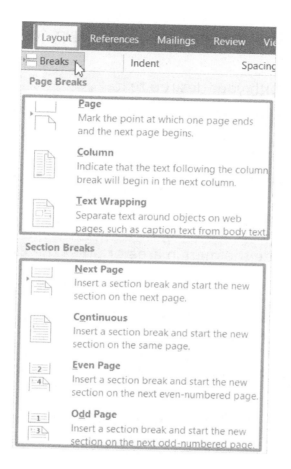

7.4 INSERTING HEADER OR FOOTER

A **Header** is a text added to the top margin of every page of a document. At the same time, a **footer** is a text added to the bottom Margin to give information about the document, e.g., the title, page number, image, logo, etc.

To add a Header or Footer to your document:

1. Go to the **Insert** ribbon.
2. Select **Header** or **Footer** command.
   A drop-down menu appears with header or footer styles.
3. Click on the desired style.

Word activates the top and bottom margin for your header or footer insertion.

4. Replace the text with your desired text.
5. Click on the **Close Header and Footer** command when you are done.

Alternatively,

1. Double-click in the top or bottom margin to activate the header and footer area.
2. Insert your footer or header.
3. Double click outside the margin area or press the **Esc** key to go back to your document.

You can always use the above method to edit your header or footer. Also available is a contextual **Design** tab you can use to design your header or footer.

To delete your header or footer, just delete the text and close the header and footer.

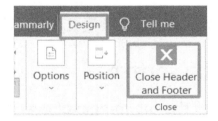

7.4.1 Inserting Different Headers or Footers in Word

To insert a separate Header or Footer for a Separate Section:

1. Insert **Next Page** section breaks to where you want different headers or footers to start.
2. Activate the headers or footers of each section.
   In the **Navigation** group of the **Header & Footer** Tools ribbon;
3. Deselect the **Link to Previous** button to disconnect the sections.

4. Add the header or footer for each section or chapter.
5. To put a different header on the first page of the document or a section, Check the **Different First Page** box.
6. To put a right-justified header for some pages and a left-justified header for some pages, check the **Different Odd & Even Pages** box.

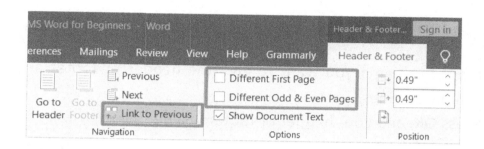

7. Close the header/footer when done with the settings.

7.4.2 Saving Headers or Footers for Later Use

In case you are using a particular header or footer to create so many documents, it will be advisable to save the header/footer.

To save your header or footer for later use:

1. Activate and select all the header or footer contents you want to save.
2. Click the **Header** or **Footer** drop-down button as the case may be.
3. Select **Save Selection to Header Gallery** or **Save Selection to Footer Gallery,** depending on whether you select Header or Footer.

A dialog box appears.

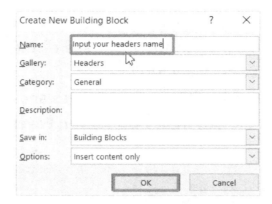

4. Input the name you want to give the header or footer and do any othe
   desired settings.

5. Press **OK,** and your header or footer will be saved.

You can access and apply the header or footer at any time in the drop-down list o
the **Header** or **Footer** drop button. You might have to scroll down to see your

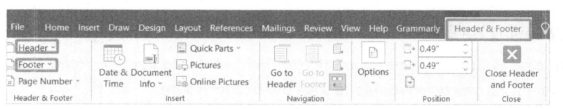

To delete your saved header or footer:

1. right-click on it.

2. Select Organize and Delete.
   A dialog box appears highlighting the header or footer.

3. Click the **Delete** button.

4. Press **yes** to confirm the prompt that appears.

5. Press **Close** in the dialog box, and your header or footer will no longer be i
   the gallery.

7.5 PAGE NUMBERING

To add page number to your document:

1. Click the **Insert** tab.
2. Click the **Page Number** button in the **Header & Footer** section.
   A drop-down menu appears with the list of where you can insert your page number.

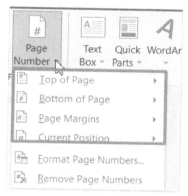

3. Select an option.
   A dialog box with page number styles appears.
4. Click your desired style.
   Word automatically adds page number to all the pages of your document and activate the header and footer area.
5. Right-click on the page number or Click the **Page Number** command in the **Headers & Footers** ribbon for settings
   A dialog box appears.
6. Select the drop-down button to select the **Number format** you want.
7. Check the **Include chapter number** box to include chapter numbers, select the **Chapter starts with style** and **Use separator** options (optional).
8. Check the **Start at** button and set the start value if you do not want the numbering to continue from the previous section (applicable for setting different page numbering for different sections).

9. Press **OK**.
10. Double click outside the margin to go back to your document area.

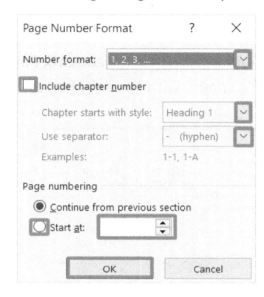

7.5.1 Inserting Different Page Numbers.

To insert different page numbers to your document:

1. Insert page number to the entire document first, following the above steps
2. Create section breaks to the document where you want different page numbers.
    If you have different chapters in your document, it is advisable to create **Next Page** section breaks for each chapter and prefatory sections. (Check **section 7.3** for the steps)
3. Double-click the header or footer of the section you want to change the page number.
4. Locate and Deselect the **Link to Previous** button in the **Navigation** group on the **Header & Footer Tools** ribbon if needs be.
5. Right-click on the page number or Click the Page Number command in the Headers & Footers ribbon to set the page numbers as desired.

6. Continue **steps 3-5** above for all the sections as desired.

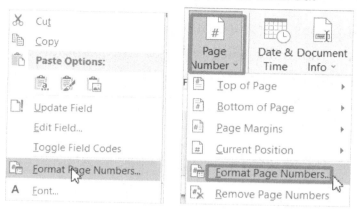

7.5.2 Removing Page Numbers.

To remove Page numbers from the entire document:

1. Go to the **Insert** ribbon.
2. Click **Page Number**.
   A drop-down menu appears.
3. Select **Remove Page Number** from the options.

Alternatively,

1. Double-click on the Header or Footer area.
2. Select the page number and press the **Delete** key.

To remove the page number from the first page of the document or a section:

1. Double-click in the margin of the section or document to activate **Headers & Footers** Tools.
2. Check the **Different First Page** box in the Options group.

You can also check the **Different Odd & Even Pages** box to remove page numbers of alternate pages.

7.6 INSERTING AUTOMATIC TABLE OF CONTENT

Microsoft Word has a feature that enables you to generate a table of content automatically or manually with easy-to-use templates. To insert a table of contents automatically in your document, you must create or format your document using the Word built-in headings in the **Styles** group (Check **section 7.1.2** for how)

To Insert a Table of Contents:

1. Ensure your document headings uses Word built-in headings styles
2. Place your insertion point where you want the table of content to be.
3. Go to the **References** ribbon.
4. Click **Table of Contents**.
   A drop-down menu appears.
5. Select an option:
   - The first two options automatically insert your table of contents with **all** your available headings.
   - The third option inserts the table of contents with placeholder texts and allows you to replace them with your own headings.
   - Select **More Tables of Contents from Office.com** for more templates.
   - Select the **Custom Table of Contents...** to customize your table. A dialog box appears, edit as desired, and press **OK**.
   - If you already have a table of content in your document, you can delete it by selecting **Remove Table of Contents.**

Updating your Table of Contents

Word does not update your table of content automatically if you make changes to your document. You will have to update it manually.

To update your Table of Content:

118

1. Position your cursor in the table of content.
   Table borders appear with buttons at the top-left.
2. Click the **Update Table** button.
   A dialog box appears.
3. Click the **Update entire table**.
4. Press **OK**.
   Word automatically updates your table.

Alternatively,

1. Right-click on the table of content.
   A drop-down menu appears.
2. Select **Update Field.** You can also select **Update Table** in the **Table of Contents** group in the **References** ribbon.
   A dialog box appears.
3. Click **Update the entire table**.
4. Click **OK**.

Note: Do not always forget to update your table after making significant changes that affect the headers or page numbers.

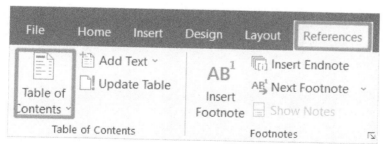

7.7 ADDING CAPTIONS TO FIGURES OR OBJECTS

A caption is a title or brief explanation of a figure or an object mostly placed below a figure or an object to give information about the figure.

To add a caption to an object:

1. Select the object you want to add a caption to.
2. Go to the **References** tab.
3. Click **Insert Caption** in the **Captions** group.

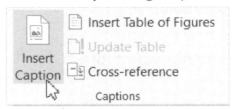

A caption dialog box appears.

4. Select **Figure** in the **Label** dropdown menu or any appropriate options.
5. Type the object description (it can include punctuations) in front of **Figure 1** in the **caption** text field.
6. Click **OK.**

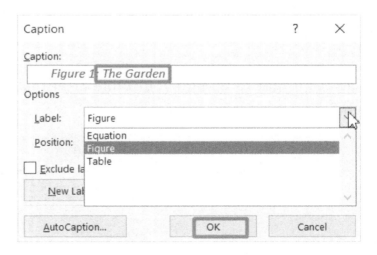

You can **format** your captions in the **Styles** group of the **Home** tab following the steps in **section 7.1**

To Add Chapter Number that updates automatically to your Image Caption.

1. Ensure you format your document headings with the Word **Headings** in the **Style** group. (Check **section 7.1** for more information).

2. Use the Word Multilevel list to number your chapter headings or **Heading 1** as the case may be following the steps below:

- Select any of your Chapters or Heading 1 style.
- Go to the **Home** tab.
- Click the **Multilevel List** icon 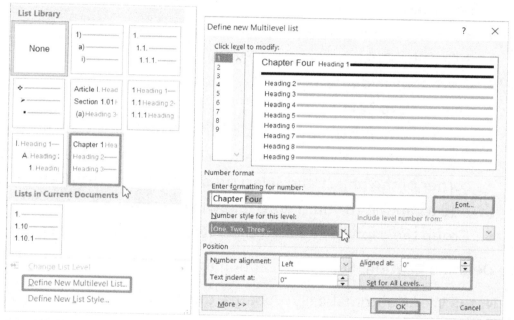 in the **Paragraph** group.
- Select **Chapter 1 Heading…,** the last option, and all Headings 1 will be numbered automatically.

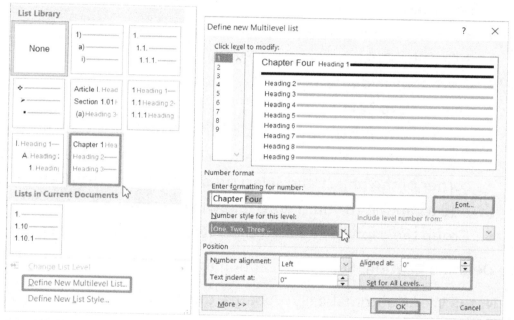

You can format the numbering in **Define new Multilevel** list. You can change the Chapter to a Section, change the numbers to words, change the font, and so on.

3. Select the object you want to add the caption.
4. Go to **References >> Captions >> Insert Caption**.
5. Select **Numbering** in the **Caption** dialog box.

A **Caption Numbering** dialog box appears.

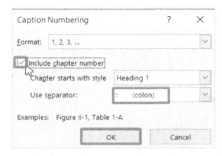

6. Check the **Include chapter number** box, select the desired separator, and press **OK**.

To make your captions sticks to your floating object:

1. Select the Object.
2. Go to the **Layout** tab.
3. Select **Wrap Text** command.
4. Choose any other options aside from the first from the dropdown list as desired. Alternatively, you can click on the Layout button at the top right corner of the object and select an option in the **With Text Wrapping** list.
5. Add a caption to your figure following the above steps.
6. Group the caption and the object (follow the steps in **section 5.13.3**)

To Delete a Caption: Select the caption and press Delete.

Note: Word automatically updates the figure numbers as you insert a new caption. You must update the caption or figure numbers whenever you delete or change the position of any caption.

To update the caption numbers:

1. Select all your document using **Ctrl + A.**
2. Right-click and select **Update Field** in the dialog box that appears **or** Press **F9** to update the caption numbers.

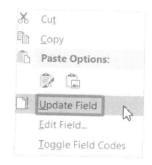

7.8 INSERTING AUTOMATIC TABLE OF FIGURES

Word has a command to automatically add a table of figures to your work, just like adding a table of contents.

For you to automatically generate a table of figures, you must have added captions to all the figures used in your document using the Word **Insert Caption** command.

To Insert Table of Figures:

1. Ensure that you use the Word caption feature to add captions to your objects.
2. Place your insertion point where you want the table of figures to be.
3. Click the **References** tab.
4. Select **Insert Table of Figures** in the **Caption** group. Table of Figures dialog box appears.

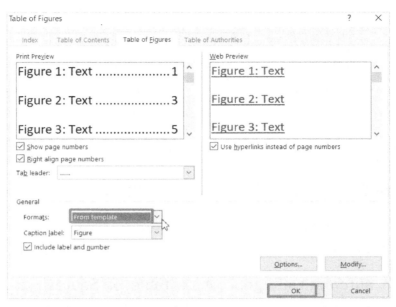

5. Select your desired Format, make other changes, preview, and press **OK** Your table of figures appears in your document.

7.9 INSERTING COVER PAGE

A cover page contains information about the document like the title, author and other enticing objects or texts.

To insert a cover page:

1. Go to the **Insert** ribbon.
2. Click the **Cover Page** button in the **Pages** group.
   A drop-down menu appears.
3. Select the desired templates to customize.
4. Edit, format, and the template to your taste. You can add images, text, and so on.

7.10 WORKING WITH CITATIONS

Citation is a way of informing the readers of the sources of your quotes or paraphrases used in your document, and it is a standard practice in academic writings. Word has a feature that helps you with the citations to save you the stress.

To insert Citation into your document:

1. Position your insertion point where you want to place your citation.
2. Click the **References** tab.
3. Click (Placeholder1) **Insert Citation** in the **Citations & Bibliography** group.
   A drop menu appears.
4. Select **Add a New Source** option.
   A dialog box appears.
5. Select the **Type of Source** (e.g., book, journal, article, etc.) using the dropdown arrow.
6. Fill in the source details in the text boxes provided.
7. Check the **Show All Bibliography Fields** for additional information.
8. Input the **Tag name**.
9. Press **OK,** and your citation is inserted.

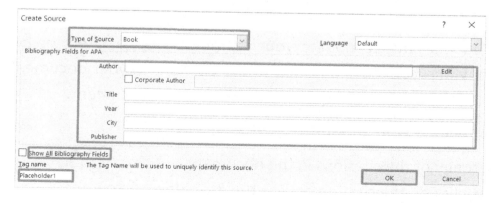

7.11 INSERTING REFERENCES, WORKS CITED, OR BIBLIOGRAPHY

References and **works cited** are alphabetical lists of all the citations used in your document, while a **bibliography** is an alphabetical list of all sources you consulted for your document, whether you cited them or not. This list is usually placed at the end of the document.

The difference between **references** and **works cited** is the format style used. There are many styles of citations by different professional and academic organizations. **References** is used when citing works that use APA (American Psychological Association) format style, and **works cited list** is used when citing works that use MLA (Modern Language Association) format style.

To insert References, Works Cited List, or Bibliography:

1. Ensure you use the Word **Citation** command to cite in your document body.
2. Place your insertion point where you want the lists to be.
3. Click the **References** tab.
4. Click **Bibliography** in the **Citations & Bibliography** group. A drop-down menu appears.
5. Select an option, and it appears in your document.

Note: You will have to update your references, works cited, or bibliography manually anytime you change or add to the citations in your document, and this can be done from the list or any of the citations in the document.

To Edit and update your citations:

- Select any of the citations in the document.
- Right-click on the citation or click the drop-down arrow.

- Select **Edit Source** from the menu that appears, edit the **Create source** dialog box, click **Ok,** and click **yes** to the prompt that appears.
- **To update**, click **Update Citations and Bibliography** instead**.**
  or
- Select the references or bibliography.
- Click on the **Update Citations and Bibliography** button at the top left corner of the list border.

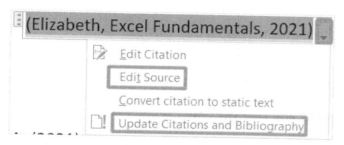

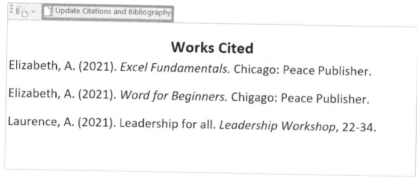

CHAPTER 8: MANAGING DOCUMENT AND WORD WINDOWS.

8.1 SAVING YOUR DOCUMENT

After creating your document, you need to save it for subsequent use or sharing.

You can save your document on your computer, in a disk drive, CD drives, USB drives, or OneDrive. Saving your work in OneDrive gives you the privilege of accessing your document anywhere you can log in to your account.

To save your document for the first time:

1. Click on the **File** tab to go to the backstage of Word.
2. Click **Save As** option in the left-side panel.
3. Select where you want to save your document in the right-side pane.
   A dialog box appears.
4. Change the document name to your desired name in the **File Name** box.
5. Select the format in which you want to save your document in the **Save as type** dropdown list.
6. Click **Save**.

You will have to save your work anytime you make changes.

To save your document subsequently,

1. Click on the **Save** icon 🖫 in the quick access toolbar or **Save** tab in the backstage view.

Alternatively,

2. use the shortcut key **Ctrl + s.**

Note: Using the above methods for the document that has never been saved will initiate the **Save as** command.

Your already saved document can also be duplicated with the same or different name and in the same or different location by selecting the **Save As** option in the Word backstage.

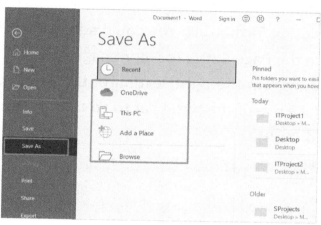

8.2 PAGE SETUPS FOR PRINTING

You can get a hard or paper copy of your document by printing.

To print your document:

1. Ensure your computer is connected to the printer.
2. Ensure your printer is loaded with the right size papers.
3. Click the **File** tab to go to the Word backstage.
4. Select **Print** in the left side pane.
   Print pane appears by the right-side.
5. Input the number of copies you want directly or with the arrows in the **Copies** box.
6. Select a printer in the **Printer** drop-down if your computer is connected to more than one printer.

7. Under **Settings**, the default settings are shown in each box. To mak
changes to any, click the drop-down in front of the one you want to chang
and select your preferred option in the drop-down menu.

- You can print specified page numbers by inputting them in the **Page**
textbox, separated by a comma.
- The paper orientation, page size, and margins appear as you have se
them during formatting. You could adjust them here if you desired.
- Click on the **Page Setup** for more page settings.

8. Preview your work in the right section of the **Print** pane to see how it wi
come out. Make use of the scroll bar to go through the pages.

9. Click the **Print** button.

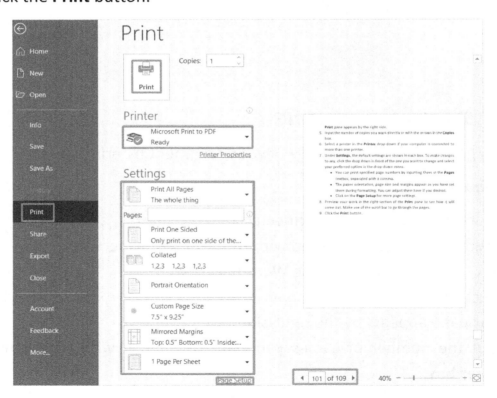

8.3 SHARING DOCUMENT BY EMAIL

Your word document can be easily shared directly as an email body or as an attachment to an email address with the **Send to Mail Recipient** command in Word. **Send to Mail Recipient** command is not available in the Word user interface by default and needs to be added. You can preferably add it to the Quick Access Toolbar by customizing it.

To add 'Send to Mail Recipient' to Quick Access Toolbar (QAT):

1. Right-click on the **QAT**.
   A dialog box appears.
2. Select **Customize Quick Access Toolbar**.
   Word Options dialog box appears.
3. From the **Choose commands from** drop-down list, choose **Commands Not in the Ribbon**.
4. Locate **Send to Mail Recipient** in the list. The list is arranged alphabetically for easy location.
5. Click **Add>>** button.
   Word adds it to Customize Quick Access Toolbar.
6. Click **OK,**
   and it appears in your Quick Access Toolbar.

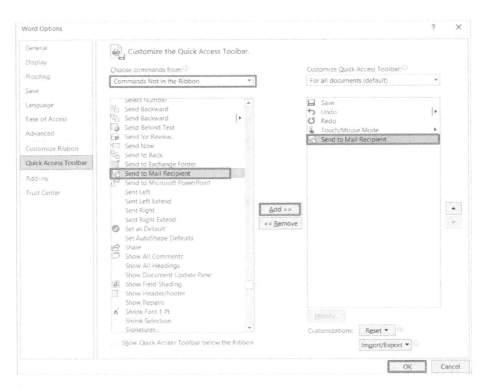

To share your document as an email body:

1. Ensure your computer is connected and sign in to your email account.
2. Click on **Send to Mail Recipient** command in the Quick Access Toolbar.
   The mail Composing window appears under the ribbon with your documen
   title already added.
3. Add the recipient's email address and other information as desired. You car
   also change the title as desired.
4. Ensure you have an internet connection.
5. Click **Send a Copy**.

Word sends your document and closes the composing email window. To close the
email window manually, click on the icon in the Quick Access Toolbar.

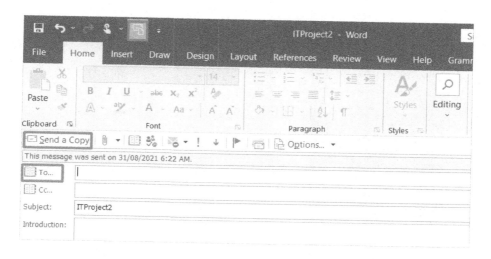

8.4 PROTECTING YOUR FILE WITH WORD SECURITY FEATURES

After devoting your time and energy to creating your document, it will be necessary to protect your sensitive document from plagiarism, stealing, indeliberate editing, and so many forms of security threats.

Word has amazing security features to help you secure your document based on how sensitive the document is.

To secure your word document:

1. Go to the Word Backstage by clicking the **File** tab.
2. Click the **Info** tab in the left side pane.
   Info pane appears on the right side.
3. Click the **Protect Document** button.
   A dialog box appears.

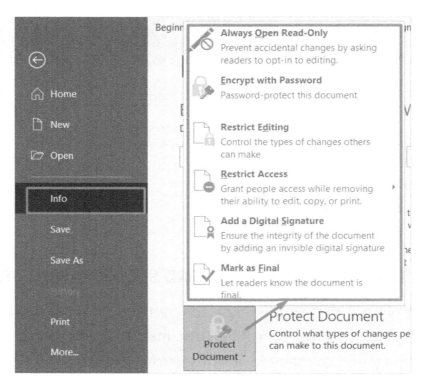

4. Select an option from the list.

- **<u>Mark as Final</u>:** This makes your document read-only (i.e., typing, editing, and proofing capabilities disabled) with a message at the top of the document screen informing the reader that the document is final. However, any reader can still edit and resave the document by clicking the **Edit Anyway** button in the top message. Select this security feature only if you just need to notify the reader that it is the recommended final version of your document or to discourage editing.

- **<u>Add a Digital Signature</u>:** Protecting your document with a digital signature has several benefits, like maintaining proof of document integrity, signer identity, and others. You must purchase a digital signature from a verified Microsoft partner to use it. Selecting this option for the first time will prompt you to where you can get one.

- **Restrict Access:** This gives people access to your document but restricts them from copying, editing, sharing, or printing your document. You will have to connect to the Information Right Management (IRM) server to help you secure the document. Selecting this option will prompt you to connect and lead you through the process.
- **Restrict Editing:** This is a flexible way of securing your document from anyhow editing and gives control over the type of editing that the allowed people can do. Selecting this option opens a pane on the right side of the document to set formatting restrictions, editing restrictions, and **start enforcement**.
- **Encrypt with Password:** Adding a password to your document is a strong form of protection, and you can give the password to only those you want to have access to your document. Nobody will be able to open your document without the password, not to talk of editing. Selecting this option, Word asks you to enter a password and re-enter it for confirmation.
- **Always Open Read-Only:** This feature prevents your document from accidental editing by always opening it as read-only. A dialog box appears each time you want to open it, notifying you that the document will be opened as read-only. Press **Yes** to continue and **No** if there is a need to make changes.
5. Follow all the prompts based on your choice and press ok.
6. Close your document for the security setting to take effect.

8.5 CLOSING YOUR WORD DOCUMENT

To close your document after you are done:

- Click the **X** button at the top-right corner of the Word window.
  Or
- Go to the **File** tab and select the **Close** option in the left-side pane.
  Or
- Use the shortcuts keys, **Ctrl + F4** or **Ctrl + W.**

Microsoft word closes or notifies you if you try to close your document without saving it.

8.6 RECOVERING UNSAVED DOCUMENT

It can happen that you mistakenly close your document without saving your last changes. The good news is that Word has an **autosave** feature that allows you to recover your file with the last unsaved changes.

To recover your unsaved documents:

1. Go to the backstage view by clicking on the **File** tab.
2. Click the **Open** tab.
   Open pane appears.
3. Click the **Recover Unsaved Documents** button at the bottom of the recently opened document list.
   The location dialog box appears with the list of unsaved documents.
4. Select the likely document. You can check the date to know the likely document.
5. Click the **Open** button.
   The document opens.
6. Save the document accordingly.

Alternatively,

1. Go to the backstage view by clicking on the **File** tab.

2. Click the **Info** tab.

  Info pane opens.

3. Select **Manage Document** dropdown.

4. Click the **Recover Unsaved Documents** menu that appears.

  The location dialog box appears with the list of unsaved documents.

5. Follow **steps 4-6** above.

8.7 OPENING SAVED DOCUMENT

You can open your document from the Word application or directly from your device.

To open an existing document from Word:

1. Go to the backstage view by clicking on the **File** tab.

2. Click the **Open** tab.

  Open pane appears.

3. Select the location of your document.

  Open dialog box appears.

4. Select the folder or your document. You can scroll down the left side list of locations on your device to locate your document.

5. Click **Open**.

Alternatively, if you recently opened your document or pinned it to Word, it will be available in the **Recent** or **Pinned** list in the backstage **Home** panel, and you can click on it to open it.

If you often use or work on your document, it will be better to pin it in Word.

To pin your document to word:

1. Locate the document in the recent list.

2. Move your cursor over the document.
3. Click the pin icon in front of the file.

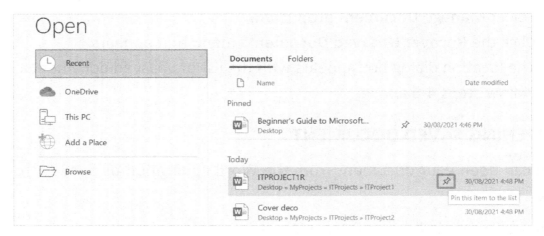

To open an existing document from your device:

1. Ensure you have the Word application installed on your computer.
2. Locate your Word document on your device.
3. Double-click to open it if it has a Word icon, if not, right-click on the file.
4. Select **open with** from the menu that appears and select **Word**.

CHAPTER 9: WORD TOP SHORTCUT COMMANDS

Working with Keyboard shortcut commands can reduce your stress, save your time and increase your productivity to a considerable extent. Below are the top shortcut commands you can use to work smartly in Word.

SN	Shortcuts	Functions
1.	Ctrl + A	To select all the content of your document
2.	Ctrl + B	To bold the highlighted contents
3.	Ctrl + C	To copy highlighted text
4.	Ctrl + D	To open a Font dialog box
5.	Ctrl + E	To center align the selected content
6.	Ctrl + F	To open the **Find Navigation** pane
7.	Ctrl + G	To open the **Go To** dialogue window
8.	Ctrl + H	To open the **Replace** dialog box.
9.	Ctrl + I	To italicize highlighted contents
10.	Ctrl + J	To justify align selected content
11.	Ctrl + K	To open the **Insert Hyperlink** dialog box.
12.	Ctrl + L	To left-align selected content
13.	Ctrl + M	To increase the Indent

14.	Ctrl + N	To create a new blank document
15.	Ctrl + O	To open an already saved document
16.	Ctrl + P	To go to **the Print** tab in the backstage view
17.	Ctrl + Q	To reset selected paragraph
18.	Ctrl + R	To right-align selected content
19.	Ctrl + S	To save your current document
20.	Ctrl + T	To increase the Hanging indent of the selected paragraph.
21.	Ctrl + U	To underline the selected text.
22.	Ctrl + V	To paste what you copied last.
23.	Ctrl + W	To close your document
24.	Ctrl + X	To cut selected content
25.	Ctrl + Y	To redo the last action, you undo.
26.	Ctrl + Z	To undo your last action
27.	Shift +Ctrl +A	To apply the All caps command
28.	Shift +Ctrl +C	To copy Format
29.	Shift +Ctrl +D	To double underline selected text
30.	Shift +Ctrl +G	To open the Word count dialog box
31.	Shift +Ctrl +J	To distribute the letters of the selected text evenly

32.	Shift +Ctrl +K	To apply the Small-cap command
33.	Shift +Ctrl +L	To apply bullet listing.

34.	Shift +Ctrl +M	To decrease Indent
35.	Shift +Ctrl +N	To apply Normal Style of the **Style** group.
36.	Shift +Ctrl +O	To open the research pane
37.	Shift +Ctrl +P	To open the Font dialog box
38.	Shift +Ctrl +Q	To set the Font to symbol.
39.	Shift +Ctrl +T	To decrease Hanging Indent.
40.	Shift +Ctrl +V	To open the Paste Format window.
41.	Shift +Ctrl +W	To underline each word of the selected content.
42.	Esc	To cancel an active command
43.	F1	To open Microsoft Word **Help**
44.	Ctrl + Alt + V	To display the **Paste Special** dialog box
45.	Ctrl + Shift + F	To open the Fonts tab of the **Format Cells** dialog box.

Made in the USA
Coppell, TX
01 February 2022

72800352R00083